Unlocking Success

A Guide to Thriving as a Dance Teacher

Nina Koch

Table of Contents

Introduction 3

Chapter 1 : Building Your Foundation 4

Chapter 2 : Crafting Your Legacy 14

Chapter 3 : Delivering Outstanding Customer Service 23

Chapter 4 : Advocating for Your Worth 32

Chapter 5 : Classroom Management and Growth 45

Chapter 6 : Continuous Learning and Evolution 55

Chapter 7 : Finding the Right Studio 65

Chapter 8 : Building Professional Connections 74

Chapter 9 : Considering Studio Ownership 84

Chapter 10 : Self-Care and Preventing Burnout 92

Chapter 11 : Effective Communication 102

Chapter 12 : Inclusivity and Accessibility in Dance 110

Chapter 13 : Leadership positions inside a dance studio and how to promote 116

Chapter 14 : Building a Personal Brand as a Dance Teacher 121

Chapter 15 : Case Studies and Guest Contributions 133

Chapter 16 : Practical Steps for Goal-Setting and Professional Development 145

Chapter 17 : Reflecting on Your Teaching Journey: Strengths, Areas for Improvement, and Growth 149

Chapter 18 : The Heart of Teaching Dance 152

Introduction

Congratulations! You want to be a dance teacher! Maybe you're a college student planning for life after graduation, transitioning from a professional dance career, or looking for ways to financially support your dance journey. Perhaps you're already teaching and want to grow, or you're figuring out how to turn your passion into a career despite others telling you that being a dance teacher isn't a "real job." Whatever your reason is, you're in the right place. This book is here to guide you, offering all the tools, advice, and steps needed to help you make your passion your profession.

Before we dive in, let me briefly introduce myself and explain why I am qualified to write this book. I am a multi-passionate entrepreneur who has been living and breathing dance for my entire life. Since 2002, I've owned multiple dance and performing arts studios, hired and trained teachers, and taught countless students who have gone on to professional careers or entered top college programs. Over the years, I've learned what makes a great studio teacher, and I'm here to show you how to build a successful and fulfilling career. I'm going to cover the exciting and the mundane and let you in on all the insider information from a studio owner who has hired and fired dozens of dance teachers over the years.

So let's dive in, but let's start from the beginning, the hiring process.

Chapter 1

Building Your Foundation

The journey to becoming a successful dance teacher begins long before you step into the studio. It starts with how you present yourself as a professional, and a big part of that is crafting a resume that highlights your skills, experience, and unique qualities. A resume is more than just a list of qualifications it's a tool that shows studio owners what makes you stand out as a teacher, a leader, and an essential part of their team. In this chapter, we'll explore how to craft a compelling resume, the key elements you should include, and why focusing on your teaching experience is just as important—if not more so—than your performance background. You'll also learn about the role you play in supporting studio enrollment and how to navigate the hiring process effectively to land your dream teaching job.

Crafting Your Dance Resume

When putting together your resume, it's easy to fall into the trap of listing all your performance achievements and expecting that to be enough. While your dance performances are impressive, what truly sets you apart as a candidate for a teaching position is your ability to convey your teaching experience. Studio owners need to know that you can effectively communicate with students, structure a class, and guide dancers of all levels to improve their skills.

Make your teaching experience the focus of your resume. Have you taught preschool ballet classes? Led hip-hop workshops for teens? Worked as an assistant teacher during summer intensives? Every bit of teaching experience counts, even if it is informal or part-time. Be specific about the age groups, levels, and genres you've taught. Studio owners look for teachers who can handle diverse groups and have the flexibility to teach various classes. Mention the number of students you typically worked with, the curriculum you followed (or created), and any notable successes you've had with your students.

If you're just starting out and don't have much teaching experience, think about ways you've been in a leadership role. Maybe you helped lead rehearsals, worked as a camp counselor, or coached a dance team. Anything that shows you can effectively manage and communicate with a group will be valuable on your resume.

One of the biggest mistakes dance teachers make when applying for jobs is focusing solely on their performance experience. While being a great performer can enhance your teaching, it doesn't automatically make you a great teacher. Studio owners know this. They are not just looking for people who can execute flawless pirouettes or breathtaking jetties; they want individuals who can inspire, educate, and mentor dancers. Your performance background is important, but it should complement not overshadow your teaching qualifications. Include it as a secondary element that shows your range of experience in the dance world, but make sure your teaching skills take center stage. When listing your performance experience, focus on how those experiences have made you a better teacher. Did your time on tour teach you discipline and time management? Did performing in a variety of genres make you a more versatile instructor? Draw connections between your performances and your teaching style.

The Key Elements of a Dance Teaching Resume

Begin your resume with your name, phone number, email address, and professional website or social media links if you have them. Make sure your email address is professional (e.g., danadanceteacher@email.com) rather than a nickname or something informal. This sets the tone that you take your role as a teacher seriously.

Include a short paragraph that summarizes who you are as a dance teacher. This is your chance to make a great first impression, so keep it concise, clear, and focused on your strengths. For example:

> "Dedicated dance educator with over 10 years of experience teaching ballet, jazz, and contemporary dance to children and adults. Passionate about fostering a supportive and inspiring learning environment, encouraging creativity, and building technical skills."

Your dance education is a critical part of your resume. List any formal training you've had, including the schools or studios you attended, programs you completed, and any certifications you hold. This can also include workshops, masterclasses, or conventions. If you trained under notable instructors or at prestigious institutions, be sure to mention that as well.

In addition, if you've attended continued education workshops or programs, list those too. This shows that you are committed to evolving as a teacher and staying current in the industry.

The most important information on your resume is your teaching experience, make this the heart of your resume. Each entry should include:

1. Studio Name & Location: The name and location of the studio where you taught.
2. Dates of Employment: The months and years you worked there.
3. Class Types & Levels: Specify what types of classes you taught (ballet, jazz, hip-hop, etc.) and the levels (beginner, intermediate, advanced). Mention age groups if relevant.
4. Responsibilities & Achievements: Highlight what you were responsible for (e.g., creating lesson plans, leading rehearsals, mentoring students, choreographing routines). Mention any notable achievements, such as students winning competitions, mastering challenging skills, or moving on to prestigious programs.

If you have taught in multiple studios, list them in order from most recent to least recent. For new teachers, list any assistant teaching roles, workshops, or leadership experiences related to dance.

Although it should not overshadow your teaching experience, your performance background is still relevant.

Keep this section brief, but include notable highlights that showcase your versatility and expertise. For example, list major productions, tours, or performances, and briefly describe your role.

If you've choreographed routines for performances, recitals, or competitions, this is an important skill to include. Be specific about the projects you've worked on and any successes you've had. For instance, did your choreography receive awards at competitions? Did you create a themed recital piece that was particularly well-received? Choreography experience indicates that you have a creative vision and can take initiative both of which are valuable to studio owners.

Studios value teachers who are dedicated to their craft and open to continued learning. Include any certifications you have, such as Acrobatic Arts, Progressing Ballet Technique (PBT), or ballroom dance qualifications. Also, list any professional development you've pursued, such as workshops, teacher training programs, or conventions. Continued education shows that you are coachable, and willing to grow and adapt, which is quite crucial in an ever-evolving industry.

Include two to three references who can speak of your teaching abilities. Make sure to ask their permission beforehand and choose individuals who have seen you teach or work directly with students. This could be previous studio owners, senior instructors, or program directors.

Your resume is your chance to show studio owners why they should hire you over other candidates. What makes you unique as a teacher? Think about your strengths, your teaching philosophy, and how you can bring something special to the studio.

Incorporate your teaching philosophy into your resume or cover letter. Are you passionate about building dancers from beginners, focusing on technique and artistry? Do you excel at fostering a fun, creative, and inclusive environment where all students feel appreciated and welcomed? Your philosophy can help studio owners see how you fit within their culture and values.

Remember, your success as a dance teacher is directly tied to studio enrollment. Your job is not only to teach but to engage students and make them excited to come back each week. This means that your work has a direct impact on the studio's revenue.

In your resume, highlight any experience that shows your ability to attract and retain students. Did you run a popular summer camp that brought in new enrollments? Did you have high attendance rates in your classes? Studio owners will be interested in your ability to elevate their business through excellent teaching that keeps students coming back.

The best time to start applying for teaching positions is in January or February. Studios are often planning their staffing needs for the next school year around this time, so it's a great opportunity to get your resume in front of decision-makers. However, studios might also be looking for summer program instructors or substitute teachers, so always keep your eyes open throughout the year.

Be ready to talk about your teaching experience and philosophy. Practice explaining your approach to different teaching scenarios. For example, how would you handle a disruptive student? How do you motivate students who are struggling? Consider these questions and prepare thoughtful, confident answers.

Some studios may ask you to teach an audition class as part of their hiring process. This is your chance to shine, so make sure you're prepared with a well-structured, engaging lesson plan. Choose exercises and activities that showcase your strengths, keep the students engaged, and allow the studio owner to see how well you interact with the class.

Just like your resume should present you as a professional, your appearance during interviews and auditions should do the same. Dress neatly and choose dance wear that allows you to move comfortably and demonstrates that you're ready to teach.

Your resume is a critical tool in building your professional image, but it's just one piece of the puzzle. When you combine a well-crafted resume with a strong teaching philosophy, a positive attitude, and a passion for dance, you become an irresistible candidate for any dance studio. Take the time to thoughtfully craft and present your skills and experiences, and you'll be well on your way to securing the teaching job of your dreams.

Building a successful career as a dance teacher requires more than just a passion for dance; it starts with how you present yourself to potential employers and students. Crafting a professional and compelling resume is a crucial step in creating this foundation. Your resume is not just a summary of your skills but a reflection of your unique qualities, strengths, and potential as a teacher. When done thoughtfully, it can help you stand out in a competitive industry and set the stage for long-term success.

Throughout this chapter, we've emphasized the importance of highlighting your teaching experience, understanding the nuances between performing and teaching, and showcasing your unique value as an educator. Studio owners are looking for individuals who can do more than demonstrate impressive dance skills; they want teachers who can communicate effectively, engage students, and foster a positive learning environment. By prioritizing your teaching qualifications, demonstrating your continued commitment to education, and clearly conveying your teaching philosophy, you position yourself as an asset to any studio.

A dance teacher's role goes beyond instructing dance steps. You play a significant part in the overall success of a studio. Your ability to connect with students, keep them motivated, and make classes engaging directly impacts student retention and enrollment. Remember that your teaching can contribute to the studio's growth and reputation. Highlighting this understanding on your resume shows studio owners that you're not just focused on teaching dance but also on being a valuable member of their team.

The dance industry is continuously evolving, and as a dance teacher, you must be willing to grow and adapt. While crafting your resume is the first step, your journey doesn't end there. Continue to seek out new opportunities to learn, whether it's through workshops, certifications, or simply observing how other instructors run their classes. Every new experience will help you refine your teaching style, build your skills, and enhance your resume over time.

Approaching the hiring process with confidence means being well-prepared and proactive. Understanding the best times to apply, preparing for interviews, and presenting yourself professionally all contribute to making a positive first impression. Remember, this is your chance to showcase not just your skills but also your enthusiasm, passion, and readiness to contribute to the studio community.

As you move forward in your career, think of your resume as a living document. Update it regularly with new achievements, classes, and professional development experiences. Each time you teach a new workshop, receive feedback from a student or attend a dance conference, you are adding to your foundation as a dance educator. These experiences shape who you are as a teacher and help define your unique style and approach.

Being a dance teacher is about so much more than sharing dance techniques; it's about inspiring students, nurturing their confidence, and helping them discover their own potential. As you work on building your foundation, remember that your passion and love for dance are at the heart of everything you do. Let this passion shine through in your resume, in your classes, and in every interaction you have within the dance community.

Your journey as a dance teacher is a continuous path of growth, learning, and creativity. Approach each step with enthusiasm, and never underestimate the impact you can make on your students' lives. By building a strong foundation, you're not just preparing yourself for a job you're setting the stage for a rewarding career that can inspire and empower others through the art of dance.

Chapter 2

Crafting Your Legacy

Being a dance teacher is about more than just teaching steps; it's about nurturing students, guiding their growth, and helping them reach their full potential. Whether your students are just beginning to learn how to shuffle or are preparing for college auditions, your role as their teacher is to be a consistent, inspiring presence in their dance journey. Crafting a lasting legacy means investing in dancers from their earliest years and watching them grow into skilled, confident performers.

As a studio owner, I can't tell you how many times teachers apply for jobs but only want to teach the advanced dancers. Everyone wants to work with the advanced students who have already mastered their technique, but finding someone who's willing to teach kids under seven can be almost impossible. (Spoiler alert, the teacher willing and able to teach the 4- 5-year-old combo class might be more valuable than the "advanced only" teacher) Here's the reality: stepping into a studio and teaching students who are already well-trained is not building a legacy. The real legacy is created by taking a 4-year-old who is licking the mirror (you laugh, but seriously, it happens) and guiding them through years of training until they become a professional-level dancer. That journey, from the very first plié to the stage, is where the magic happens.

It's easy to see why teaching advanced dancers is appealing. They already know the basics, they understand your corrections, and they're eager to learn complex choreography. But if you want to build a career that's fulfilling and sustainable, you need to embrace teaching students at all levels, especially beginners. Teaching young, beginner dancers is where you have the greatest opportunity to make a long and lasting impact. These are the students who will remember you as the person who introduced them to the world of dance and set them on their journey.

Teaching young children can be a unique and joyful experience. You're not just teaching them dance steps; you're teaching them how to listen, how to move their bodies, and how to express themselves. You're planting the seeds of confidence, discipline, and creativity that will grow over time. Each small victory whether it's mastering a tendu or learning to stay focused during class is a step forward, and you get to be the one who guides them through it.

When you take the time to build a strong foundation with beginners, you're setting them up for success. As they progress, they'll carry the skills you taught them into every class they take, and that's what makes a great dancer. You're not just helping them learn the basics; you're giving them the tools they'll need to excel for years to come.

If you're looking to work full-time at a studio, you can't expect to do so only by teaching advanced dancers. No studio can offer full-time hours just for teaching upper-level classes; the demand simply isn't there. Combo classes those that combine different dance styles or cater to younger age groups are the lifeblood of any dance studio. These classes are where students begin their dance journey, and they're often the most popular, drawing in new students and helping to build a studio's enrollment.

Combo classes typically introduce young children to two or more styles of dance within a single session. For example, a class might include 30 minutes of ballet followed by 30 minutes of tap. These classes are designed to be fun, engaging, and educational, giving children a taste of multiple styles without overwhelming them. For many kids, combo classes are their first experience with dance, and they set the tone for how they'll feel about dancing in the future.

Teaching combo classes may not sound as glamorous as leading an advanced pointe class, but it's essential for the success of the studio and your career as a dance teacher. Combo classes are often the first point of entry for new students. If children have a positive experience, they're more likely to stick with dance, leading to higher retention rates and more filled classes across all levels. Because combo classes are so popular, they tend to fill up quickly, providing more teaching opportunities. This consistency can lead to a more stable and sustainable schedule for you as a teacher.

Teaching beginners means you're responsible for building the foundation of a dancer's training. A solid foundation is crucial for a dancer's future success, and it starts with you.

By taking on this role, you're shaping the future of the studio and the students who will grow up there. Teaching combo classes requires a special set of skills. You need to be able to engage young children, maintain their attention, and make learning fun. It's about understanding how to break down steps into easy, manageable parts and using language that kids can understand. If you can master the art of teaching combo classes, you'll become an invaluable asset to any studio.

Creating a legacy isn't about a single class or a single season; it's about long-term growth. The most rewarding experiences often come from teaching a dancer over many years and seeing them develop from a shy, uncertain beginner to a confident, skilled performer. This kind of growth takes time, patience, and dedication, but it's also what makes teaching so fulfilling.

When you teach young beginners, you have the opportunity to shape their journey from the very beginning. You're not just teaching them how to dance; you're teaching them how to be students, how to work hard, and how to enjoy the process of learning. Every correction, every word of encouragement, and every smile helps them grow not just as dancers, but as individuals.

Some of the most rewarding moments in a dance teacher's career come when students who started as beginners are accepted into college dance programs, join professional companies, or return to teach at the studio where they started. Knowing that you played a vital role in their success is incredibly fulfilling, and it's what drives many teachers to continue doing what they do.

Think about the impact you can have over the course of a student's dance journey. If you teach a child for 10, 12, or even 15 years, you've not only helped them develop their technique but also guided them through some of the most formative years of their life. You've taught them discipline, teamwork, perseverance, and how to express themselves creatively. These are lessons that will stay with them long after they leave the studio, and that's how you build a legacy.

Teaching young children is both a challenge and a joy, requiring patience, creativity, and adaptability. Young dancers come with short attention spans, boundless energy, and a touch of unpredictability, which makes every class a unique experience. Keeping them engaged can be difficult, but it's also essential for their learning. It takes creativity to design classes that are fun and interactive, ensuring that their attention is fully captured and held. Patience is another key factor, as each child learns at their own pace. Some may pick up skills quickly, while others need more time to master certain movements. Being able to adapt your teaching style to suit each child's individual needs is crucial, as what works for one student may not work for another.

Despite these challenges, the rewards are worth it! One of the most fulfilling aspects of teaching young children is watching their growth over time. Seeing them improve their skills, gain confidence, and eventually perform at recitals is a special privilege that makes all the hard work worthwhile. Dance class often becomes a place where children build confidence, form friendships, and learn to express themselves. As their teacher, you have the chance to be a positive influence in their lives, which is a powerful and rewarding responsibility. Additionally, by nurturing beginners, you are playing a critical role in creating the next generation of dancers. Whether they pursue dance professionally or continue as a hobby, you've helped instill a lifelong love for the art. Investing your time and talent into the youngest dancers in the studio also makes you an asset to the Studio Owner.

When you're willing to teach beginners, you set yourself apart as a teacher who can handle the full spectrum of what a dance studio needs. This makes you more valuable because you're flexible, versatile, and committed to nurturing all students, not just the ones who are already advanced. Studios thrive when they have teachers who are passionate about building dancers from the ground up, and that's where your opportunity lies.

Your ability to work with different age groups, skill levels, and dance styles will make you a stronger candidate for future opportunities. Studio owners are always looking for teachers who can adapt, take on various classes, and contribute to the studio's overall success. By developing your skills in teaching beginner and combo classes, you're building a well-rounded teaching portfolio that showcases your versatility.

Teaching young children often means forming strong relationships with their parents, who are typically very involved in their child's activities. When parents see that their child is excited about class and making progress, they're more likely to continue enrolling them. This creates a stable, long-term client base for the studio. Your ability to engage both students and parents is a huge asset to the studio and will contribute to your success as a Legacy Dance Teacher.

Crafting a legacy as a dance teacher isn't just about creating beautiful choreography or teaching advanced techniques it's about the relationships you build, the lives you touch, and the passion for dance that you cultivate in your students. Your legacy is defined by the dancers you help shape from their very first plié to their final bow, and by the lessons you impart that go beyond the dance floor. Teaching dance is an investment in your students' futures, and the rewards come not only from watching them grow as dancers but also from knowing you played a huge role in their personal development.

The willingness to teach beginners, especially young children, is at the core of building a meaningful and lasting career in dance education. When you choose to work with those who are just starting their journey, you are choosing to plant seeds that will grow into something extraordinary over time. The skills you teach them, the confidence you build, and the love for dance you instill in them will shape their future, whether they continue to pursue dance as a career or simply carry the joy of dance throughout their lives.

It's easy to focus on the immediate gratification that comes from working with advanced dancers, but the true measure of a teacher's impact lies in the long-term development of their students. The next generation of dancers, choreographers, and even future dance teachers all start as the little ones learning to skip, twirl, and find the beat. Your role as a teacher of beginners is not just to instruct but to inspire and ignite a passion that will drive them forward.

A dance teacher's legacy doesn't fade when a recital ends or when students graduate from the studio. It lives on in the memories, skills, and experiences that students carry with them. Many dancers look back fondly on the teachers who nurtured them when they were young, who believed in them when they doubted themselves, and who pushed them to reach for more. By embracing the opportunity to teach at all levels, especially beginners, you're creating the kind of legacy that leaves a lasting impact not just on the dance floor but in the hearts of your students.

The world of dance is ever-evolving, and the future of this art form depends on teachers who are dedicated to nurturing young talent and encouraging a love for dance that will carry on for generations. When you commit to guiding students from their very first steps, you're not just teaching dance—you're shaping the future of the dance community. Your dedication to helping dancers grow is what will keep the art of dance vibrant and continuously thriving.

By focusing on long-term growth, embracing the challenges and rewards of teaching beginners, and contributing to the overall success of the studio, you are building a career that is both fulfilling and sustainable. You are also becoming an integral part of a community that values creativity, discipline, and the joy of self-expression. This is the true essence of a dance teacher's legacy creating a foundation upon which the future of dance can stand strong and flourish.

As a dance teacher, you are entrusted with the incredible responsibility and privilege of shaping the lives of your students. You have the power to influence how they see themselves, how they face challenges, and how they find joy in movement. When you invest your time, energy, and passion into teaching beginners, you are doing so much more than teaching dance steps; you are giving them the confidence to explore new things, the resilience to overcome difficulties, and the joy of finding a community where they belong.

Every class you teach, every word of encouragement you offer, and every correction you make contributes to your legacy. Whether your students go on to become professional dancers, and choreographers, or simply carry a love for dance throughout their lives, your impact is profound and lasting. Embrace the opportunity to teach students of all levels, and take pride in knowing that you are not just teaching dance you are crafting a legacy that will be felt for years to come.

Chapter 3

Delivering Outstanding Customer Service

Dance studios are part of the service industry, and like any service-based business, customer satisfaction is key to success. As a dance teacher, you are not only responsible for teaching steps, choreography, and technique; you also play a major role in the overall customer experience. I am going to introduce you to Mike Michalowicz, a business author and coach, Queen Bee Role, the QBR.

Mike Michalowicz's "Queen Bee Role" (QBR) concept, which he introduces in his book Clockwork, is all about figuring out what the most important activity in your business is the one thing that absolutely drives its success. He compares it to a beehive, where the queen bee's main job is to lay eggs. While the queen bee is essential, it's not the bee herself that's most important, but the role she plays laying eggs to keep the hive growing and thriving. Every bee in the hive works to support and protect that role, because without it, the hive would collapse.

For a business, the Queen Bee Role is that critical task or function that everything depends on. In a dance studio, the most important job is to deliver engaging, entertaining, and educational classes. These classes are the "queen bee" role the lifeblood of the studio. Without them, the studio would fail. As a dance teacher, you are responsible for delivering the queen bee role, and you have a massive influence on the success and sustainability of the studio. Your classes drive enrollment, retention, and ultimately the studio's revenue. You're not just teaching dance you're selling an experience. But this doesn't mean selling in a pushy or "used car salesperson" kind of way. Instead, your role is to diligently engage, inspire, and build relationships so that students and parents feel connected to the studio and want to come back year after year.

Your classes are the products the studio sells. Parents enroll their children in dance because they want them to learn, grow, and have fun. If your classes aren't engaging, students will lose interest, and parents will stop paying for lessons. On the other hand, if you're delivering an outstanding experience, students will look forward to every class, and parents will see the value in continuing their child's enrollment.

When new students come to try a class, that trial is your opportunity to convert them into regular students. You're not selling by pushing a product; you're selling by creating a positive and memorable experience. If the student has fun, feels welcomed and enjoys your teaching style, they are much more likely to sign up for ongoing classes. This is where your role as a teacher overlaps with sales. The better the experience you create, the more likely it is that new students will want to join your classes.

When a new student comes to try a class, they are evaluating whether this is something they want to commit to. As a teacher, your job is to make that trial class an exceptional experience. It's not just about impressing the student it's about showing both the student and their parents why your class is worth their time and investment.

Think about how you can make a strong first impression. How do you greet new students? How do you introduce yourself and make them feel welcome? Be warm, approachable, and enthusiastic. Explain what they can expect from the class, and make sure they feel comfortable. If they're nervous, reassure them that it's okay to take things at their own pace.

Your energy sets the tone for the class. If you're enthusiastic, energetic, and clearly enjoying what you're doing, your students will pick up on that and have a better time. For new students, it's especially important to create an environment where they feel like they can relax, have fun, and be themselves.

Make an effort to give each student some individual attention during class, especially new students who might feel unsure. A small correction, a word of encouragement, or even just calling them by name can make a huge difference in how comfortable and included they feel. When parents see that you're attentive and care about their child's progress, they're more likely to enroll them in your class.

Don't let the connection end when the trial class is over. Encourage parents to ask questions and make sure they know how to enroll if they decide to join. A friendly follow-up can reinforce the positive experience and show that you're genuinely interested in having their child as part of your class.

Your "sales" job doesn't end there, once a dancer is enrolled we want them to stay, long term. Retention is when a dancer signs up year after year.

Retention is equally as important as recruitment. You might have a lot of new students coming in, but if they aren't staying, the studio isn't growing. Retention is about keeping your current students engaged, excited, and challenged so that they want to keep coming back. This is achieved by building relationships, showing genuine interest in each student's progress, and maintaining a high level of energy and enthusiasm in every class.

One of the most effective ways to retain students is to build strong relationships with them and their families. Make a point to greet parents when they drop off or pick up their children. Let them know you're paying attention to their child's progress by sharing small successes or asking if they have any questions. When parents see that you're invested in their child's growth, they're more likely to see the value in continuing lessons. You may not have thought about this before but, delivering curriculum, giving kind and thoughtful corrections, investing in relations with your dancers and their families is good customer service.

While the term "customer service" might not be the first thing that comes to mind when you think of a dance teacher, it's a critical part of the job. Parents are your customers, and your students are the reason they're there. Making sure that both feel satisfied with the experience you provide is essential for the studio's success.

As a dance teacher, you're part of a team that's delivering a service. The parents pay for classes, and they expect a high level of quality. They want to see their children learning, having fun, and improving. By delivering on these expectations, you're helping to build trust and loyalty between the families and the studio.

Every interaction you have with students and parents is an opportunity to create a positive experience. Whether it's greeting them when they arrive, offering encouragement during class, or giving feedback after a recital, your goal is to make them feel valued and appreciated.

Sometimes, things don't always go as planned. A student might be struggling, a parent might have concerns, or you might need to handle a class with fewer students than usual. Part of delivering outstanding customer service is knowing how to handle these challenges professionally and gracefully. If a parent expresses a concern, listen to them, acknowledge their feelings, and offer a solution if possible. If a student is having a difficult time, find a way to support and encourage them without disrupting the rest of the class.

Part of your delivery of the QBR and a high level of customer service is you, your dancers expect to see you every week so consistent, exemplary attendance is key to your success as a dancer teacher. But, dance teachers, like everyone, have days when they need to take time off. Whether it's due to illness, a family event, or other commitments, it's important to handle absences professionally. Missing class is sometimes unavoidable, but there are steps you can take to minimize the impact on your students and the studio.

If you need to miss a class, it's your responsibility to find a substitute. Having a reliable network of fellow teachers who can step in when needed is invaluable. If your studio has a process for finding substitutes, make sure you follow it. It's important that classes run as smoothly as possible even in your absence, and that requires communication and planning.

Make sure your substitute has everything they need to teach the class. Provide a lesson plan, notes on any choreography they need to cover, and any special instructions they should be aware of. This will help ensure that your students still have a productive, enjoyable class even when you're not there.

While everyone needs time off now and then, it's best to keep absences to a minimum. Consistency is important for your students, and frequent absences can disrupt their progress. When you're reliable and present, it reinforces the idea that you're committed to their development.

While maintaining consistent attendance is key to supporting your students' progress, the true mark of a successful dance teacher goes beyond just being present. It's about creating a long-lasting impact on all your students, not just those with exceptional talent.

A true testament to the skill level of a teacher is not measured by how successful their naturally talented dancers are, real success comes from cultivating and engaging dancer's long term who will be mid-level recreational dancers forever. How do we do this? We remember what matters. Only around 3% of dance students will become professionals so lets focus on the many positive life skills dance offers. Dance offers so much more than just steps and technique. It teaches valuable life skills like discipline, confidence, teamwork, and perseverance. As a dance teacher, you have the opportunity to inspire your students in ways that go beyond the studio.

Learning dance requires focus, practice, and discipline. By setting clear expectations and encouraging students to work hard, you're teaching them skills that will benefit them in all areas of life. Whether they're practicing a new combination or preparing for a recital, they learn the value of dedication and perseverance.

Dance can be an incredible confidence booster. Performing on stage, mastering a challenging routine, or even just dancing in front of peers can help students feel more confident in themselves. As a teacher, your encouragement and support play a huge role in building that confidence. Celebrate their successes, big and small, and help them see how far they've come.

Dance is often a team effort. Whether it's a group routine or a recital, students need to learn how to work together, communicate, and support each other. By encouraging teamwork and fostering a sense of community in your classes, you're helping students develop essential social skills.

Dance is a form of artistic expression, and it gives students the chance to express themselves in ways that words can't always capture. Encourage your students to explore their creativity and find their own unique voice through movement. While fostering creativity and encouraging your students to express themselves through dance is crucial, your role as a teacher extends far beyond the artistic aspects. Being a successful dance teacher also means understanding the business side of running a studio, where customer service plays a key part.

Delivering outstanding customer service as a dance teacher is about much more than just being friendly and professional. It's about creating a positive, engaging experience that keeps students excited to come back to class. By understanding the critical role you play in recruitment, retention, and customer satisfaction, you can help build a strong, thriving dance community.

Remember, every time you step into the studio, you're not just teaching dance you're delivering the Queen Bee role. You're creating memories, building relationships, and inspiring a love of dance that will last a lifetime. Keep serving your students with passion, dedication, and joy, and you'll not only see them thrive, but you'll also find your own sense of fulfillment as a dance teacher.

Chapter 4

Advocating for Your Worth

If we want to elevate the dance industry and ensure it thrives, we need to treat dance studios like the businesses they are and make sure that dance teachers are compensated fairly and legally. As a dance teacher, understanding your rights, your worth, and the legal framework surrounding employment is essential. This chapter will cover wage negotiation, labor laws, and the benefits of aligning yourself with studios that value and support their staff. By understanding how to advocate for your worth, you can help create a healthier, more professional, and sustainable dance industry for yourself and future generations of teachers.

One of the most critical aspects of advocating for your worth as a dance teacher is understanding your employment status. I need to preface all of this by saying, I am not a lawyer. I am just using the information I know to help you reach your goals. If you have questions about your employment status or options, reach out to your state employment development office.

In many states, including California, it is not legal for you to be classified as an independent contractor if you are working regular, scheduled classes at a studio. However, many dance teachers find themselves being paid this way without fully understanding the implications. So, what's the difference?

When you are classified as an employee, your studio owner is required to:

- Pay employment taxes (Social Security, Medicare, unemployment insurance).
- Provide you with a W-2 form for tax purposes at the end of the year.
- Ensure that you are covered by worker's compensation insurance.
- Adhere to state labor laws, which may include minimum wage requirements, overtime pay, and mandatory sick leave.

As an employee, you also pay into Social Security and Medicare, which will benefit you later in life. You may have access to unemployment benefits if you lose your job, and you're also protected if you are injured while working. This means that if you or your partner becomes pregnant, you may be eligible for disability insurance benefits during your leave.

If you are classified as an independent contractor, you are essentially running your own business. This means you are responsible for:

- Paying self-employment taxes, which are often higher than what you'd pay as an employee.
- Covering your own insurance, including health and liability.

- Securing your own worker's compensation, as you are not protected under the studio's insurance.
- Filing your own taxes as a business entity, which can be more complicated.

In this setup, you do not have access to unemployment benefits, paid sick leave, or protection if you are injured on the job. While independent contractors do have more flexibility and control over their schedules, the lack of security can be a significant drawback.

Being classified as an employee offers greater legal protection, security, and benefits. If your studio treats you as an independent contractor but controls your work hours, provides a consistent schedule, and directs how you teach your classes, they may be misclassifying you, which could be illegal in many states. This misclassification not only puts you at risk but also limits your ability to access important benefits like Social Security, disability insurance, and worker's compensation.

While I'm not a lawyer, it's important to have a basic understanding of the labor laws that apply to dance teachers, especially if you live in states like California where the rules are very specific. Each state has its own set of laws, so be sure to research what applies where you teach; but here are a few general principles to keep in mind:

1. Mandatory Sick Leave:
   In California, even part-time employees are entitled to a mandatory 24 hours of paid sick leave each year. This means that if you're classified as an

employee, you should be accruing paid sick time. Some states have similar laws, and others may even offer more extensive benefits. Make sure you understand your rights and check with your studio owner to see how this applies to you.

2. Overtime Pay:
Each state has rules about when overtime kicks in, and it's essential to know whether you are eligible. For example, in California, you must be paid overtime (1.5 times your regular rate) if you work more than eight hours in a day, more than 40 hours in a week, or working 7 days in a row without a day off regardless of how many hours are worked. It's crucial to ensure you're being compensated correctly.

3. Worker's Compensation Insurance:
One of the biggest benefits of being classified as an employee is that your studio is legally required to carry worker's compensation insurance. This insurance protects you if you are injured while teaching or rehearsing, covering medical expenses and providing compensation if you're unable to work for a period of time. If you're classified as an independent contractor, you won't have access to this safety net, which means you're taking on much more risk.

4. Social Security and Unemployment Benefits:

As an employee, you and your employer both pay into Social Security. This is the program that provides benefits if you retire, become disabled, or need financial assistance after losing a job. If you're classified as an independent contractor, you'll need to pay into these programs yourself, and the self-employment tax rate can be significantly higher. Additionally, as an independent contractor, you won't have access to unemployment benefits if your studio decides to cut your classes or close down.

5. State Disability Benefits:
In some states, disability benefits may also be available to employees. This can be incredibly important if you need to take time off for a medical condition, pregnancy, or injury. Disability benefits provide a partial income replacement while you recover, but it may only be available if you're classified as an employee.

6. State Unemployment Benefits:
State unemployment benefits are financial support programs provided by state governments to individuals who have lost their jobs through no fault of their own. These benefits are designed to help workers during periods of unemployment by offering temporary financial assistance while they search for new employment. The benefits are funded through payroll taxes that employers pay into the unemployment insurance system.

For dance teachers, being hired as "employees" rather than "independent contractors" is crucial in order to be eligible for state unemployment benefits. Here's why:

1. **Eligibility for Unemployment Benefits**:
   Unemployment benefits are typically only available to individuals classified as employees. Employees are entitled to unemployment compensation when their employment is terminated, as long as they meet certain eligibility criteria (e.g., sufficient work history and reason for job separation). Independent contractors, on the other hand, are considered self-employed and are generally not eligible for unemployment benefits.

2. **Employer Contributions**:
   Employers are required to pay into the unemployment insurance system for their employees. These contributions are based on payroll taxes and are mandatory for every business with employees. This ensures that employees can access unemployment benefits if they are laid off or their job is eliminated. Independent contractors do not receive these benefits because employers do not pay unemployment taxes for them.

3. **Job Security and Protection**:
   Dance teachers who are classified as employees are afforded legal protections, including access to unemployment benefits, workers' compensation, and other employee rights like minimum wage and overtime pay. If a dance studio experiences a

downturn in enrollment or makes staffing changes, employee dance teachers can rely on unemployment benefits to support them financially while they search for new work.

4. **Unforeseen Circumstances**:
Dance teachers often face challenges such as seasonal shifts in class attendance or studio closures (like during the COVID-19 pandemic). If hired as employees, teachers have a safety net through unemployment benefits that can help them get through these tough times, offering financial support while they find new opportunities

5. **Financial Security:**
Unemployment benefits provide a financial cushion, helping teachers pay bills and cover essential expenses if their work is unexpectedly reduced or eliminated. As employees, dance teachers need to be assured they are protected in case their income is disrupted.

As a dance teacher, it's essential to advocate for yourself by ensuring you're hired as an employee rather than an independent contractor. Being classified as an employee gives you access to crucial unemployment benefits, which can provide financial support if you ever lose your job. This classification also protects your job security, giving you access to important legal protections like workers' compensation and other employee rights.

Don't settle for being labeled as a contractor you deserve the protections and stability that come with being an employee.

Negotiating Your Wage: Knowing Your Worth

Knowing your legal rights is essential, but so is understanding your value as a dance teacher. Studios are businesses, and like any business, they need to pay for the services they receive. Your time, expertise, and passion are valuable assets, and you deserve to be compensated fairly for them.

However, your pay and raises are not solely tied to how good your dancers or dances are. Your studio should have a list of Key Performance Indicators (KPI) and Key Results Areas (KRA) that measure your success as a teacher.

Sample KRA and KPI for Dance Teachers

A Key Result Area (KRA) is defined as something for which you are completely responsible. This means that if you don't do it, it doesn't get done. A **key result area** is an activity that is under your control. It is an output of your work that becomes an input or a contributing factor to the work of others.

KRAs-
- Classroom Management
- Student Progress
- Choreography
- Retention/Attrition
- Conversion

- Responsibility and Responsiveness (as it relates to deadlines and internal studio communication)
- Creative contribution to the growth of your program and the business.

A **Key Performance Indicator (KPI)** is a measurable value or tangible result that demonstrates how effectively you are achieving key business objectives. **Key Performance Indicators** are used to evaluate your success in your work at the studio.

KPIs-
1. Well run and **orderly class**: students understand studio rules and the discipline policy is enforced. Lessons are planned in advance. Classes start and end on time and class time is balanced and used wisely.
2. Students learn the material as outlined in the **curriculum** and demonstrate increased mastery of skills from the start of a session to the end of a session.
3. **Recital dances** are clean, creative, and showcase curriculum skills.
4. **Retention** from one session to the next and attrition during the session will be measured. Our studio-wide goal is 70% retention from June/July to the beginning of the new season in August, but your goal inside a dance year should be to retain 100% of the students you start the year with until the end of June/July.
5. Your **conversion rate** is the percent of potential students who try your class that enroll in your class. This will be measured throughout the year.

6. **Deadlines** are met and all internal studio **communications** are responded to within 48 hours. You work independently and take care of your studio responsibilities with minimal assistance from the admin and leadership team. Accurate attendance is entered weekly.
7. **Share ideas** for ways to grow and improve your program/classes. **Contribute and participate** in our closed staff Facebook group

Before you start negotiating, do some research to understand what the standard pay rates are for dance teachers in your area. Rates can vary widely depending on location, experience, and the type of classes you teach. Reach out to other teachers, look online, or attend industry events to get a sense of the going rates. Knowing what other studios are paying can help you negotiate a rate that is competitive and fair.

Your experience, training, and expertise all contribute to your worth. Do you have specialized training or certifications? Are you particularly skilled at teaching a certain age group or style of dance? Can you help with choreography, recitals, or other special projects? These skills can all add value to your role at the studio, and they should be reflected in your pay.

If you're negotiating a contract or pay rate, be clear about what you need. This might include a higher hourly rate, paid time off, health benefits, or reimbursement for travel expenses. Being upfront and honest about your expectations helps to set the tone for a professional relationship where both parties feel respected.

It can be scary to turn down a job offer, but sometimes it's necessary. If a studio is unwilling to pay a fair rate or treat you as an employee when you should be classified as one, you have the right to walk away. While this may not always be possible, especially when you're just starting out, knowing when to say no can be empowering and may encourage studios to reassess their practices.

Not all studios are created equal. Some treat their teachers as valuable team members, while others see them as replaceable. When looking for a job, it's essential to align yourself with studios that value and support their staff. Here's how to find a studio that will support your growth and well-being:

If a studio is run like a business, it's more likely to adhere to legal requirements and treat its staff fairly. A well-organized, professional studio will have systems in place for payroll, contracts, and employee benefits. It's a red flag if a studio seems disorganized or unwilling to provide information about your employment status and compensation.

During your interview, ask about the benefits the studio offers. Are you classified as an employee? Is there paid sick leave? Does the studio provide or reimburse for professional development opportunities? Studios that are committed to supporting their teachers will have answers to these questions, and they'll be upfront about what they can offer.

A studio's culture can make a huge difference in your experience as a teacher. Are the owners supportive and communicative? Do they encourage collaboration among teachers? Do they value continuing education and encourage you to develop your skills? Finding a studio that aligns with your values and provides a positive work environment can make all the difference in your job satisfaction.

It's not enough to know your worth; you also need to protect your time and well-being. Teaching dance can be physically and emotionally demanding, and it's important to set boundaries to avoid burnout.

Make sure you're clear about your availability and the hours you're willing to work. If you're constantly taking on extra classes or working outside of your availability, you may quickly find yourself overwhelmed. Setting boundaries isn't about being inflexible, it's about taking care of yourself so that you can continue to teach and inspire your students.

As a dance teacher, your body is your tool. Make sure you're taking care of yourself by getting enough rest, eating well, and staying active. If you need to take time off to recover from an injury, illness, or other health issue, don't be afraid to do so. Remember, as an employee, you have the right to sick leave and other benefits that can help you during these times.

Teaching can sometimes feel isolating and draining, especially if you're working multiple gigs at different studios. Building a network of fellow dance teachers can provide support, advice, and a sense of community. Whether you connect online, attend local events, or join a professional association, having a support network can make advocating for your worth a little bit easier.

Advocating for your worth as a dance teacher is about more than just negotiating a pay rate. It's about understanding your rights, building strong professional relationships, and ensuring that you're treated fairly in the workplace. By aligning yourself with supportive studios, understanding your employment status, and taking care of your well-being, you can create a fulfilling, sustainable career.

Ultimately, when dance teachers advocate for fair treatment and compensation, it helps elevate the entire industry. It sets a higher standard and encourages more studios to operate professionally, creating a healthier, more sustainable dance community for everyone. So don't be afraid to stand up for your worth, protect your rights, and contribute to the positive growth of the dance world.

Chapter 5

Classroom Management and Growth

Setting the right tone in your classroom is essential for success. This chapter explores effective techniques for establishing boundaries with students and parents, maintaining focus, and creating a positive learning environment. Learn how to set the pace and standard in your classroom, and why having a lesson plan or curriculum can elevate your teaching.

Setting the right tone in your classroom is one of the most critical aspects of being a successful dance teacher. A well-managed classroom is not only about maintaining order; it's about creating an environment where students feel supported, engaged, and inspired. Effective classroom management allows you to teach more effectively, helps your students learn more efficiently, and establishes a positive and productive atmosphere. This chapter explores essential techniques for establishing boundaries with students and parents, maintaining focus, and setting the pace and standard in your classroom. We'll also discuss why having a lesson plan or curriculum is crucial for your success and how it can help you navigate unexpected challenges.

Setting boundaries is essential for creating a classroom environment that fosters respect, focus, and growth. It starts with making sure everyone students and parents alike understands the stated rules and expectations. Clear, consistent boundaries help to build trust and make your role as the leader of the class unmistakable.

Boundaries are the foundation of effective classroom management. Without them, it's easy for the atmosphere to become chaotic, and once control is lost, it's challenging to regain. Setting clear boundaries helps students understand what is expected of them and creates a space where they can thrive. When students know the rules and feel safe, they are more willing to take risks, try new things, and focus on learning.

1. Start with Clear Communication:
   At the beginning of each term or session, clearly explain the rules and expectations for your class. This includes how students should behave, how they should treat each other, and what the consequences will be if rules are broken.

2. Lead by Example:
   As the teacher, you set the tone. If you show respect, patience, and enthusiasm, your students are more likely to mirror those behaviors. Consistency is key; students should see that you mean what you say and that rules apply to everyone.

3. Consistent Enforcement:

Enforcing rules consistently is crucial. If you overlook a behavior one day and react to it the next, students will become confused about what is acceptable and not. Be firm but fair, and follow through with the consequences you've established.

4. Involve Parents When Necessary:
   If a student's behavior is consistently disruptive, don't hesitate to communicate with their parents. Make sure to approach these conversations with a solution-oriented mindset. Explain what the issue is, how it's affecting the class, and how you can work together to address it.

One of the most important aspects of classroom management is setting the pace and standard. As a dance teacher, you are the leader from the moment you step into the studio. There is a leadership role open in every class, and it's your job to fill that spot immediately. If you don't, one of your students will take that leadership position, and it can lead to the class spiraling out of control.

Your students are looking to you for direction. If you walk into the room without a plan, asking your students what they want to work on today, you're giving them control of the class. This can lead to confusion, lack of focus, and a loss of productivity. You need to walk in with confidence, ready to lead, and make it clear that you are in charge of the class.

This may sound simple, but the way you present yourself can have a significant impact on how your students perceive you. Dress in a way that reflects your role as a leader and professional. If you walk in looking disorganized or casual, it can send a message that you're not serious about your role, and students may be less likely to take you seriously.

You set the standard for behavior, effort, and focus. If you want your students to arrive on time, prepared, and ready to work hard, you need to model that behavior. Start your class on time, come prepared, and bring enthusiasm and energy to your teaching. Your students will follow your lead, and over time, you'll establish a culture of excellence in your classroom.

While modeling high standards and leading by example are key to creating a positive classroom environment, working with teens requires an added layer of clear boundaries. As students grow older, they need structure and guidance more than friendship. Maintaining professionalism helps you establish authority and create an environment where teens can thrive under your leadership. By setting these boundaries, you ensure that trust and respect remain at the core of your teaching, allowing your students to feel supported while you maintain effective control of the class.

Teaching teens can be rewarding, as long as you are addressing the class in a way to keep expectations clear. Teen students need guidance, structure, and support, not a friend. Trying to be "cool" or overly friendly can blur the lines of your authority and make it harder to manage your class effectively. Teens are at a stage where they need someone who can lead and inspire them, not someone who wants to be their buddy. Maintain professionalism, show respect, and keep your interactions appropriate. This will help build a sense of trust and mutual respect. Your best tool in your tool box to set the class tone and expectations in your lesson plan.

Walking into a class without a plan is one of the quickest ways to lose control. Students can sense when you're not prepared, and it can lead to confusion, lack of focus, and behavioral issues. Having a solid lesson plan helps you maintain control, stay on track, and ensure that your class runs smoothly.

A lesson plan is your roadmap for the class. It allows you to structure your time, set clear objectives, and ensure that you're covering everything you need to. With a plan in place, you can confidently guide your students through the lesson, even if unexpected challenges arise. Lesson plans also give you the flexibility to make adjustments as needed without losing your focus.

No matter how well-prepared you are, things don't always go as expected. Maybe a piece of equipment is missing, the music isn't working, or a student is struggling with a particular step. That's why it's essential to have a backup plan. Having alternative exercises or activities ready can help you navigate unexpected challenges without losing momentum.

In addition to your lesson plan, think about your overall goals for the class. What do you want your students to achieve by the end of the term? Share these goals with your students and involve them in the process. Ask them what their personal goals are and incorporate those into your plan. When students have clear goals, they are more motivated, focused, and fully engaged.

Having a curriculum in place can elevate your teaching by providing a long-term plan for your students' progress. A curriculum ensures that your classes build on each other, helping students develop their skills consistently over time. It also allows you to track their progress and identify areas where they need more support. Developing your own curriculum or following one provided by the studio can add structure to your teaching and give students a clearer sense of their own growth.

One of the biggest challenges in teaching is keeping students focused and engaged, especially when working with younger children. It's easy for students to get distracted, but there are techniques you can use to keep their attention.

Children, especially young ones, learn best when they're having fun. Use creative imagery, storytelling, and games to make your lessons more engaging. For example, if you're teaching pliés, you can pretend that the students are opening a window or growing like trees. This helps them connect with the movement in a way that's fun and memorable.

Breaking down your lesson into smaller, manageable segments can make it easier for students to stay focused. Start with a warm-up, then move to technique, then choreography, and end with a cool-down. Keep each segment relatively short and switch things up to keep their interest.

Now that we've covered the importance of structured lesson plans and how they provide the foundation for an organized and effective class, it's time to focus on another essential element of teaching praise. While structure guides the flow of learning, praise is what motivates and encourages students to push themselves further. Recognizing and celebrating progress, no matter how small, plays a crucial role in building confidence and fostering a positive learning environment. Let's explore how praise can uplift your dancers and help them reach their full potential.

Praise and encouragement are powerful tools for maintaining focus. When students know that their hard work will be recognized, they are more likely to stay engaged. Be specific with your praise, such as, "I loved how you pointed your feet during that combination," instead of just saying, "Good job." Specific feedback helps students understand what they're doing right and encourages them to keep putting in the effort.

While specific praise and encouragement are great tools to keep your students motivated and engaged, it's also important to recognize when a lack of focus stems from physical or mental fatigue. Students, especially those who have had a long day at school, may struggle to maintain concentration. In these moments, incorporating short, active breaks can give them the chance to refresh and refocus, helping them return to the lesson with renewed energy and attention. Let's explore how simple movement breaks can make a big difference in keeping your class on track.

Incorporating short, active breaks during your class can be a game-changer for keeping students focused and energized. These breaks don't have to be long or complex just a few moments where students can stretch, shake out their limbs, or take a few deep breaths can make a significant impact. These small pauses allow their bodies to release built-up tension and their minds to reset, helping them return to the lesson with a renewed sense of energy and concentration. It's especially helpful for students who've spent long hours in school and are feeling mentally or physically drained.

Additionally, these active breaks can serve as a moment to refocus the entire class. For example, after a particularly challenging combination or a detailed correction, a quick stretch or breathing exercise can help your students absorb the feedback without feeling overwhelmed. This practice not only re-energizes the group but also creates a structured way to transition between different sections of the class, ensuring that focus is maintained throughout the lesson. Incorporating these mindful moments makes the class more dynamic and helps you maintain an engaging, productive environment.

Even with the best preparation, there will be days when things don't go smoothly. Whether it's a student having a meltdown, a parent who's upset, or technical difficulties, handling these situations with confidence and grace is key to maintaining control of your classroom.

When faced with a challenging situation, the most important thing is to stay calm. If you react with frustration or panic, it will only escalate the situation. Take a moment to breathe, assess the situation, and respond calmly and confidently.

If a student is being disruptive, address it right away. Letting small issues slide can lead to bigger problems down the line. Use clear, direct communication to explain why the behavior is unacceptable and what the consequences will be if it continues. Be firm but respectful, and make sure you're consistent in how you handle these situations.

Sometimes, addressing classroom issues may involve communicating with parents. Approach these conversations with a positive and collaborative attitude. Let them know you're invested in their child's success and that you're looking for solutions. Share any concerns you have and ask for their input on how to address the situation.

Effective classroom management is about more than just controlling behavior. It's about creating an environment where students feel supported, motivated, and inspired. By setting clear boundaries, establishing a positive tone

Remember, you are the leader in the room. Your students look to you for guidance, and the way you present yourself sets the tone for the entire class. Walk in with confidence, clarity, and a plan, and your students will follow your lead. Whether you're teaching toddlers or teens, your ability to manage your classroom will determine not only how well your students learn but also how much they enjoy the experience.

So, come in with your lesson plan, be ready to lead, and inspire your students with every class you teach. With the right approach, you can create a classroom culture where students feel challenged, supported, and eager to grow.

Chapter 6

Continuous Learning and Evolution

As a dance teacher, your education should never stop. The world of dance is constantly evolving, with new styles, techniques, and teaching methodologies emerging all the time. To stay relevant and effective, you need to commit to continuous learning. This chapter emphasizes the importance of ongoing education through workshops, certifications, and evolving teaching methods. By staying updated on the latest trends and expanding your skill set, you'll be better equipped to adapt to the changing needs of your students, keep your teaching fresh, and inspire the next generation of dancers.

The dance industry is dynamic. What was popular and effective five or ten years ago might not be relevant today. As new techniques, teaching philosophies, and styles emerge, it's essential for dance teachers to stay informed and open to growth. Continuing education is not just about learning new dance steps; it's about refining your approach, understanding your students better, and exploring new ways to engage and inspire them.

Continuous learning is essential in the dance world because it allows you to stay adaptable and relevant in an ever-changing field. By keeping up with industry advancements, you can maintain a deep connection with your students and avoid falling behind. Expanding your skill set through workshops and continued education not only makes you a better dancer but also enhances your versatility as a teacher. Learning new methods of movement and instruction gives you the tools to reach more students in different, impactful ways.

Additionally, every student brings unique challenges and learning styles to the classroom. What works for one dancer may not resonate with another. By continuously broadening your knowledge, you can better meet the diverse needs of your students and find creative solutions to help them overcome obstacles and stay engaged. This constant growth also boosts your confidence in the studio, as you'll feel more prepared to handle a wide range of teaching scenarios. Furthermore, having certifications and ongoing training under your belt will elevate your credibility as a teacher, making you more desirable to studios and parents alike. Continuous learning isn't just about improving your skills it's about maintaining your edge in a competitive industry.

There are many ways to keep your dance education ongoing. Whether it's attending workshops, obtaining certifications, or simply connecting with other teachers and professionals in the industry, continuous learning will keep your skills sharp and your teaching fresh.

Workshops and conventions are excellent opportunities to learn new techniques, try different dance styles, and network with other professionals. Many of these events are taught by renowned industry experts, giving you access to knowledge and insights that you might not get elsewhere. Workshops can range from one-day intensives to multi-day events, and they often include a variety of classes, panels, and networking opportunities.

Certifications can help deepen your expertise in specific areas of dance, such as acrobatics, ballet technique, or dance conditioning. Programs like Alixa Flexibility and Acrobatic Arts offer certifications that can enhance your teaching and give you new skills to bring back to your studio. Certifications demonstrate that you've invested in your education and are committed to maintaining high teaching standards.

While in-person workshops are invaluable, online learning has made continuing education more accessible than ever. There are countless webinars, video courses, and online classes that allow you to learn from the comfort of your home. If you can't travel to attend a workshop, online resources are a great alternative. Many organizations now offer virtual conferences and training sessions, making it easier than ever to access expert instruction.

Learning from a mentor can be one of the most rewarding ways to grow as a dance teacher. A mentor can provide guidance, answer your questions, and help you navigate challenges in your teaching career. They can also introduce you to new ideas and techniques, pushing you to think more creatively about how you teach. If you're struggling to find your own mentor, consider reaching out to teachers you admire or attending events where you can connect with experienced professionals.

Continuing Education Opportunities: Where to Start

Are you lost trying to find continued education opportunities? Here is a list of trusted programs, mentors, and events that can help you take your teaching to the next level:

More Than Just Great Dancing - Teacher Training

More Than Just Great Dancing (MTJGD) offers a variety of training programs for dance educators. Their approach focuses on not only teaching technique but also building a supportive and professional studio culture. MTJGD has a strong emphasis on leadership and business skills, making it ideal for teachers who aspire to grow within their studios or even open their own.

Dance Teacher Summit

The Dance Teacher Summit is one of the most popular events in the industry. It brings together dance teachers from around the world for a multi-day conference filled with workshops, panel discussions, and networking opportunities. You'll have the chance to learn from some of the best teachers and choreographers in the world, pick up new teaching methods, and get inspired by other professionals who share your passion.

Dance Teacher Web

Dance Teacher Web provides online resources, webinars, and events for dance teachers of all levels. Whether you're looking to learn new choreography, explore teaching tips, or find business advice, Dance Teacher Web has a wealth of information to help you grow. They also host an annual conference that includes masterclasses, seminars, and networking events.

Rhee Gold's DanceLife Teacher Conference

Rhee Gold's DanceLife Teacher Conference is designed specifically for dance educators. The event covers everything from technique and choreography to studio management and marketing. It's a fantastic opportunity to connect with other teachers, learn from experienced professionals, and gain new perspectives on teaching.

Alixa Flexibility

Alixa Flexibility offers a certification program focused on safe and effective stretching techniques. Flexibility is a crucial component of dance, and Alixa's program teaches instructors how to help their students improve their flexibility while reducing the risk of injury. This certification is particularly valuable for teachers who work with competitive dancers or students looking to enhance their technique.

Acrobatic Arts

Acrobatic Arts is a certification program that specializes in teaching acrobatics within a dance context. Their courses cover everything from basic acro skills to advanced techniques, with a strong emphasis on safety and progressions. Acrobatic Arts certification can help you expand your class offerings, attract new students, and teach acro skills with confidence.

Godfrey Method

The Godfrey Method, a pioneering approach in dance education, was established by Jonathan and Chelsea Godfrey. Its roots trace back to our early work with our own dancers, where years of meticulous development laid the foundation for what it is today. Officially founded in 2020, The Godfrey Method emerged as a beacon of innovation and resilience in the dance world. With the dance community grappling with vulnerability and the sudden shift away from traditional, in-person training during the 2020 pandemic, we, Jonathan and Chelsea, delved deep into research. Our goal was clear: to foster growth and learning in our students despite the constraints.

Day to Day Dance Teacher

The mission of DaytoDay Dance Teacher is to provide positive solutions to dance struggles. We strive to educate fellow dance educators and dancers in safe and effective training. DaytoDay Dance Teacher was born because of the need in the dance community for dancers and teachers to have access to tailored training programs, consulting, choreography, and education.

The Ballet Blog

The Ballet Blog is your ultimate guide to resolving pain, preventing injury, and optimizing dance performance. The information provided here is designed to help you optimize your body's biomechanics and provide the tools you need to empower you in your own healing.

After exploring the many continuing education opportunities available to dance teachers, it's important to understand why these experiences are vital to your professional growth. As dance is an ever-evolving art form, new trends, techniques, and teaching methods emerge regularly. Participating in ongoing education ensures that you stay current with these changes, allowing you to effectively adapt your teaching to meet the demands of today's dance students. By continuously refining your skills and learning new approaches, you not only maintain your own growth as a teacher but also provide your students with the most relevant and inspiring training possible.

To be an effective dance teacher, you need to be willing to adapt and evolve. The dance industry changes quickly, and what worked five years ago might not be effective today. Students today have different needs, expectations, and learning styles than they did in the past, and it's essential to stay responsive to these shifts.

Dance styles evolve over time, influenced by culture, music, and the media. Over the 3 decades of my own teaching experience I have seen shifts in culture, teaching techniques, dance technique and dancer safety. As a teacher, it's important to stay current with these changes so you can continue to teach your students accurately and effectively.

As dance styles, culture, dancers learning styles, and needs continually evolve, so too must the methods we use to teach them. Staying current with these changes ensures that you can provide your students with an up-to-date and accurate learning experience. However, keeping pace with evolving trends in dance isn't just about mastering the latest movements it's also about understanding how your students learn. Recognizing that every dancer processes information differently, adapting your teaching methods to accommodate various learning styles is just as essential. By combining your knowledge of evolving dance trends with diverse teaching strategies, you can ensure that every student has the opportunity to thrive.

No two students are the same. Some learn best by watching, others by doing, and still others by listening. Being aware of different learning styles and adapting your teaching methods accordingly can make a big difference in how effectively your students learn. Continuous education can introduce you to new ways of presenting material, different methods of breaking down techniques, and creative ways to keep students engaged.

Adapting your teaching methods to accommodate different learning styles is key to helping each student reach their full potential. By continuing to expand your knowledge and finding new ways to engage students, you create a more inclusive learning environment. At the same time, embracing modern technology can further enhance your teaching approach. From virtual classes to video analysis, integrating technology allows you to not only reach a wider range of students but also to offer more interactive and efficient ways of teaching. Combining varied teaching methods with innovative tools ensures that your classes remain dynamic and accessible to all learners.

Technology has become an integral part of teaching, and there are countless ways to incorporate technology into your teaching. Online platforms can help you connect with students who can't attend in person, video recordings can help students review choreography, and apps can assist with everything from music editing to lesson planning. Staying open to new technology can help you reach more students and make your teaching more efficient.

Committing to continuous learning doesn't just make you a better teacher; it also benefits your career. Studios are always looking for teachers who are well-trained, adaptable, and committed to their craft. By investing in your own education, you make yourself more marketable and open up new career opportunities.

Studios value teachers who bring a wide range of skills and expertise. The more you can offer, the more indispensable you become. If you can teach multiple dance styles, work with different age groups, and bring new ideas to the studio, you'll be more likely to secure and maintain a stable teaching position.

Every time you attend a workshop, earn a certification or learn something new, you're investing in your professional growth. This kind of continuous improvement can lead to more opportunities, such as teaching advanced classes, choreographing for special performances, or even training new teachers.

The dance industry is a community, and when you invest in your own education, you're also investing in the community. You can bring new ideas back to your studio, share knowledge with your colleagues, and contribute to the overall growth of the industry. A stronger, more knowledgeable community of teachers means a better learning environment for students everywhere.

Teaching dance is a journey, not a destination. The most effective and inspiring teachers are those who continue to learn, adapt, and grow throughout their careers. By committing to continuous education, you're not just improving your own skills you're helping to elevate the entire dance community.

So take advantage of the resources, workshops, and opportunities available to you. Seek out mentors, try new things, and be willing to step outside your comfort zone. The more you learn, the more you can bring back to your students, and the more rewarding your teaching career will be. Keep your mind open, your skills sharp, and your passion for dance alive, and you'll find that there's always something new to discover on your journey as a dance teacher.

Chapter 7

Finding the Right Studio

Your success as a dance teacher can be greatly influenced by the studio where you work. The environment, culture, and values of a studio shape not only your experience as a teacher but also your professional growth and job satisfaction. Choosing the right studio can make all the difference between a fulfilling, stable career and a frustrating, unfulfilling job. This chapter will guide you through the essential elements that make a great studio, from professionalism and core values to growth opportunities, helping you find a place that aligns with your goals and treats you as a valuable member of the team.

Every studio has its own unique culture, management style, and approach to teaching. Some studios emphasize competition, while others focus on community performances, and others may specialize in a specific dance style. Understanding what kind of environment you thrive in and what aligns with your teaching philosophy is crucial for your long-term success and happiness.

The culture of a studio directly impacts how you teach, interact with students, and develop your career. A supportive and professional culture will encourage you to grow, learn, and become the best teacher you can be. On the other hand, a poorly managed studio with unclear expectations or a lack of support can leave you feeling undervalued and stressed. Finding a studio that fits your personality and values can help you build a rewarding, sustainable career.

When you work at a studio that aligns with your values and offers opportunities for growth, you're more likely to feel satisfied and motivated. Job satisfaction isn't just about the pay; it's about feeling supported, respected, and valued as a professional. The right studio will invest in your growth, encourage your ideas, and make you feel like an integral part of the team.

Before you can find the right studio, you need to understand what you're looking for. This means reflecting on your career goals, teaching style, and personal values. Here are some questions to consider:

What Are Your Career Goals?

Are you looking to build a long-term career at a studio, or are you looking for part-time work while pursuing other interests? Do you want to specialize in teaching one style, or would you prefer to teach a variety of classes? Defining your career goals will help you identify which studios are a good fit and which ones may not meet your long-term needs.

What Kind of Teaching Environment Do You Thrive In?

Think about the type of students you enjoy working with and the teaching environment that suits you best. Do you enjoy working with competitive dancers, or do you prefer a more relaxed, recreational environment? Would you rather teach young beginners, advanced dancers, or a mix of all levels? Knowing what kind of environment brings out your best will help you find a studio where you can thrive.

What Are Your Core Values?

Your core values will play a significant role in determining where you feel comfortable and motivated. Consider what matters most to you: professionalism, creativity, a sense of community, or a focus on personal growth. Identifying your values will help you seek out studios that align with them, creating a more harmonious work environment.

Now that you've defined what you're looking for, let's explore the key elements that make a dance studio great. These are the factors that will contribute to your success, growth, and satisfaction as a dance teacher.

Professionalism

A great studio operates like a business. This means that they have clear policies, contracts, and expectations for both teachers and students. Professionalism ensures that you're paid on time, treated fairly, and have a clear understanding of your role. Studios that lack professionalism often have issues with communication, scheduling, and management, which can lead to a chaotic work environment.

What to Look For:

- Clear contracts outlining your pay, hours, and responsibilities.
- Transparent policies regarding class cancellations, absences, and substitute teaching.
- Regular communication from studio management about schedules, events, and updates.
- Respectful treatment of teachers and staff.

Core Values

The core values of a studio reflect what they prioritize and believe in. A studio that values creativity, for example, might encourage teachers to experiment with choreography and bring new ideas to the table. A studio that values community might focus on creating a supportive environment where all students feel welcome. Working for a studio with strong, positive core values can make your job more meaningful and enjoyable.

What to Look For:

- A clear mission statement that outlines the studio's goals and values.
- An environment that fosters respect, inclusivity, and creativity.
- A studio culture that aligns with your own values and teaching philosophy.
- Support for initiatives that promote student growth, community involvement, and teacher development.

Growth Opportunities

A great studio will invest in your growth as a teacher. This might include opportunities to attend workshops, learn new styles, or take on leadership roles within the studio. Growth opportunities are essential for maintaining your enthusiasm and helping you advance in your career. If a studio is willing to invest in your development, it's a sign that they value your contributions and see you as a long-term part of their team.

What to Look For:

- Opportunities to attend training sessions, workshops, and conferences.
- Access to mentorship or guidance from more experienced teachers or studio owners.
- The chance to take on new classes, projects, or leadership roles.
- Encouragement to develop your own curriculum or bring new ideas to the studio.

Stability and Security

Job stability is crucial, especially if you're looking for a long-term career at a studio. A great studio will have a solid business model, a steady flow of students, and a reputation for being well-managed. Stability means you can focus on teaching without constantly worrying about job security.

What to Look For:

- A well-established studio with a steady enrollment of students.
- Positive reviews and a good reputation in the community.
- Clear and consistent payment schedules.
- A history of retaining teachers and students.

Respect and Communication

Respect and open communication are the cornerstones of a positive work environment. You want to work at a studio where your voice is heard, your concerns are properly addressed, and your contributions are appreciated. Studios that foster respect and communication create a sense of teamwork and belonging.

What to Look For:

- Management that listens to your feedback and is open to new ideas.
- Regular staff meetings to discuss schedules, events, and any issues that arise.
- A respectful atmosphere where teachers are treated as professionals.
- Clear and timely communication about changes, updates, and expectations.

How to Research and Evaluate a Studio

Before accepting a position, do your research. The more you know about the studio, the better equipped you'll be to make an informed decision. Here are some steps you can take:

1. Visit the Studio in Person:
   Ask to observe a class or take a tour of the studio. This will give you a sense of the environment, the way classes are run, and how the studio is managed. Pay attention to how teachers and students interact, and observe the overall atmosphere

2. Talk to Other Teachers:
   If possible, talk to other teachers who work at the studio. Ask them about their experiences, how they feel about the management, and whether they enjoy working there. This can provide valuable insights that you won't get from just talking to the owner.

3. Check Online Reviews and Social Media:
   Look up the studio's website, social media pages, and online reviews. This will give you a sense of how the studio is perceived by the community. Positive reviews from parents and students are a good sign, while consistently negative reviews might be cause for concern.

4. Ask Questions During the Interview:
   Don't be afraid to ask questions during your interview. Inquire about the studio's values, opportunities for growth, how they handle conflicts, and what their expectations are for teachers. The

answers you receive can help you determine whether the studio is a good fit for you.

The key to finding the right studio is aligning your goals, values, and teaching style with what the studio has to offer. A studio that encourages creativity, supports professional development, and fosters a positive work environment will allow you to grow, thrive, and build a rewarding career. Don't settle for a studio that doesn't treat you with respect or provide opportunities for growth; instead, seek out a place that sees your potential and wants to help you succeed.

If you're looking to build a long-term career, find a studio that aligns with your vision for the future. Are they expanding? Do they have plans to open new locations? Are they looking for teachers who can take on leadership roles? Studios that are growing and evolving are more likely to offer you stability and opportunities to advance.

Finally, trust your instincts. If something doesn't feel right, take the time to explore your concerns. Sometimes, the culture of a studio can be hard to define on paper, but if your gut tells you it's not the right place for you, it's okay to keep looking.

Finding the right studio is one of the most important steps you can take in building a successful and fulfilling career as a dance teacher. By identifying what you want, understanding what makes a studio great, and doing your research, you can find a place that aligns with your goals and values. A studio that treats you with respect, supports your growth, and values your contributions will not only make your job more enjoyable but also help you reach your full potential as a teacher.

Remember, you deserve to work in an environment where you feel valued and respected. Don't settle for less. Take the time to find a studio that truly appreciates your skills, shares your vision, and is committed to helping you grow. The right studio can make all the difference, turning a job into a rewarding, inspiring career.

Chapter 8

Building Professional Connections

Some of this is repetitive, however, that is how important I think this subject is!

Teaching dance isn't just about the steps, the music, or the choreography it's about building connections. The relationship you build with your students can have a profound impact on their growth, confidence, and love for dance. But there's a fine line between building strong, supportive relationships and crossing into unprofessional territory. Establishing clear boundaries with your students and their parents is crucial, not just for your professional integrity but also for your emotional well-being and safety. This chapter will explore how to navigate these relationships, especially when working with teens, and how to foster an environment of trust and respect while maintaining appropriate boundaries.

As a dance teacher, you play many roles in your students' lives. You're a mentor, an instructor, a coach, and sometimes even a role model. The relationships you build with your students are a key part of what makes your teaching effective, as they create a sense of trust, motivation, and comfort that allows students to grow. However, it's essential to remember that you are still their teacher not their friend. Establishing boundaries is critical for maintaining professionalism, ensuring safety, and protecting yourself emotionally.

Boundaries help create a safe, respectful, and productive environment in your classroom. They define the limits of acceptable behavior and ensure that both you and your students understand the nature of your relationship. Without boundaries, lines can easily blur, leading to misunderstandings, discomfort, and even safety concerns. For dance teachers, maintaining clear boundaries is particularly important because of the close, physical nature of the work.

Building trust with your students is essential, but it doesn't mean you need to be their friend. Trust comes from showing respect, demonstrating expertise, and creating a consistent, fair, and supportive environment. Students should feel comfortable approaching you with questions or concerns, but they should also understand that there are limits to how personal the relationship can become.

One of the biggest challenges for dance teachers, especially when working with teens, is maintaining appropriate boundaries. Teens can be incredibly fun to teach, but they can also be tricky to navigate because they are at a stage in life where they are forming their identities and often testing boundaries. They might see you as a friend, confidant, or role model, but it's essential to remind yourself (and them) that you are still their teacher.

Your students, whether they are children or teens, are still navigating the complexities of emotional and social development. No matter how mature they may seem, it's essential to remember that they are not your peers. Building friendships with your students can blur the line between teacher and authority figure, making it harder to maintain respect and discipline within the classroom. It can also lead to potential misunderstandings or safety concerns, especially when professional boundaries are not upheld.

The most critical reason for maintaining these boundaries is to ensure the safety and integrity of both you and your students. When relationships become overly personal, it opens the door to misinterpretations that could compromise your professional reputation. By keeping clear lines of separation, you safeguard your role as a teacher and create a structured, safe environment where students can thrive.

Furthermore, maintaining authority is vital for effective classroom management. When students start seeing you as a friend rather than a teacher, it becomes difficult to enforce rules and maintain discipline. Students who view their teacher as a peer are less likely to respect instructions, which can quickly lead to classroom disruptions.

Lastly, clear boundaries foster a healthy learning environment. Students, especially younger dancers, need structure and guidance to feel secure in their learning space. Knowing that there are defined boundaries helps them focus on their growth and development, rather than navigating unclear personal dynamics. By modeling appropriate behavior and professionalism, you set the tone for respect and responsibility, creating an environment where students can flourish academically and personally.

Tips for Maintaining Boundaries with Students

1. Keep Communication Professional: Avoid texting students directly. If you need to communicate outside of class, do so through official channels like email or the studio's communication platform, and keep the messages focused on dance-related topics.

2. Be Mindful of Physical Contact: Dance often involves physical adjustments, but it's crucial to be respectful and professional when making corrections. Always explain what you're doing and ask for permission when needed. This not only ensures that your students feel comfortable but also reinforces the idea that you are there in a professional capacity.

3. Avoid Sharing Personal Details: It's okay to share aspects of your life, such as your dance background or favorite dance memories, but avoid discussing personal issues, relationships, or other private matters. Students don't need to know about your personal life, and oversharing can make it difficult to maintain boundaries.

4. Model Appropriate Behavior: Set the tone for how you expect your students to interact with you and each other. If you maintain a professional demeanor, your students are more likely to treat you with the respect you deserve.

After establishing clear boundaries with your students by maintaining professional communication, being mindful of physical contact, and modeling appropriate behavior, it's essential to recognize that each age group presents its own unique challenges. While these tips help create a respectful and professional environment, working with teens requires a slightly different approach. As they go through a pivotal stage of self-discovery, they may start seeing you as more than just a teacher. Balancing their need for guidance and mentorship while maintaining clear professional boundaries is key to creating a healthy and productive learning environment. Let's explore how to navigate these tricky dynamics with teen students.

Teaching teens can be one of the most rewarding parts of being a dance teacher, but it also comes with its own set of challenges. Teens are navigating a critical period of self-discovery, and they may see you as a mentor, role model, or even a friend. While it's great that they feel comfortable around you, it's important to remember that they are still your students, not your peers.

It can be tempting to try to relate to your teenage students by acting like a friend, but this is a dangerous path. The closer you get to a student, the harder it becomes to enforce rules, give constructive criticism, or maintain authority. It can also lead to misunderstandings or inappropriate behavior, even if it starts with the best of intentions.

Being professional doesn't mean you can't be warm, friendly, or approachable. It means understanding where the line is and making sure you don't cross it. Teens need boundaries, even if they act like they don't. They need to know that while you care about them, there are certain limits to the relationship. Maintaining professionalism ensures that everyone knows their role and understands what is appropriate.

Teens often face issues they might not want to talk to their parents about, and they may see you as someone they can trust. If a student confides in you about a problem, listen empathetically, but be careful about how you respond. Remember that you are not a therapist, and there are limits to what you can and should handle. If a student's issue is serious, encourage them to speak to their parents or a professional, and consider notifying your studio management if you're concerned about the student's well-being.

Similarly, it's crucial to maintain professional boundaries with parents. Building positive relationships is essential to your success, but parents may sometimes blur the line between professional and personal interactions, especially when it comes to their child's progress. Keeping these boundaries in place will help you manage expectations and maintain fairness in the classroom. Let's explore how to navigate these relationships with parents while keeping things professional.

Building connections with parents is crucial for a successful teaching career, but it's important to keep those connections professional. Parents are often very invested in their child's success, and it's easy to fall into a trap where they try to befriend you, hoping for special treatment or favors for their child. While it's natural to want to build positive relationships, maintaining clear boundaries is essential.

Parents will often act like your friend as long as things are going well for their child. They may compliment your teaching, bring you gifts, or chat with you after class. But it's important to recognize that these actions don't necessarily mean genuine friendship. If a parent's child doesn't get the part they want in a production, or if there's a conflict, that "friendship" can quickly turn. Keeping a professional distance protects you from the emotional ups and downs that can come with trying to be too close to parents.

It can be heartbreaking when a parent you thought you had a good relationship with suddenly becomes hostile or dismissive because their child didn't get what they wanted. This is why maintaining boundaries is so important. By keeping things professional, you can protect yourself from getting emotionally invested in relationships that may not be as genuine as they seem.

Tips for Maintaining Professional Boundaries with Parents

1. Keep Conversations Dance-Focused:
   When chatting with parents before or after class, keep the conversation centered on dance-related topics. Avoid discussing personal issues, gossip, or other matters that aren't directly related to your work.

2. Use Professional Communication Channels:
   Just like with students, it's best to communicate with parents through official channels. If a parent reaches out to you via text or social media, kindly redirect them to email or the studio's preferred communication method.

3. Be Fair and Consistent:
   Treat all students and parents equally, regardless of how well you know them. Avoid showing favoritism, and make sure your decisions about casting, class placement, and other matters are based on merit and consistency.

4. Stand Firm in Difficult Situations:
   If a parent becomes confrontational or tries to push boundaries, remain calm and professional. It's okay to say no, and it's okay to enforce studio policies. If needed, involve studio management to help mediate the situation.

Now that we've covered some practical tips for maintaining professional relationships with parents, it's important to understand how these efforts contribute to building trust. Trust is the foundation of any successful teacher-parent relationship, but it isn't established through friendliness alone it's built on professionalism, consistency, and knowledge. When parents see that you are reliable, fair, and genuinely invested in their child's development, they are more likely to respect your role and decisions. This trust, in turn, fosters a positive environment in which both students and parents feel confident in your guidance and leadership.

Establishing trust is at the heart of building positive, professional connections with your students and their parents. Trust doesn't come from being a friend; it comes from showing that you are reliable, knowledgeable, and consistent. When students and parents trust you, they are more likely to respect you, listen to your feedback, and engage positively with the studio.

One of the best ways to build trust is to be consistent in your behavior, teaching, and communication. When students and parents know what to expect from you, they feel more comfortable and secure. This doesn't mean you can't be flexible or adapt to new situations, but it does mean that your overall approach should be steady and reliable.

If a student is struggling, be honest with them (and their parents) about what they need to work on. If a parent asks a question you don't know the answer to, admit it and offer to find out. Transparency builds trust, and it shows that you are confident in your role as a professional.

Your classroom should be a safe space for all students, where they feel respected, supported, and encouraged to grow. By setting clear boundaries and leading by example, you create an environment where students can thrive. When students know they are in a safe, structured space, they are more likely to open up, take risks, and push themselves to new levels of achievement.

Building professional connections is about more than just managing behavior or enforcing rules; it's about creating an environment where trust, respect, and learning can flourish. By establishing clear boundaries with your students and parents, you can protect your professional integrity, maintain a safe classroom environment, and ensure that your relationships are built on respect and mutual understanding. Remember, as much as you care about your students, they are not your friends. They need you to be their teacher, their guide, and their mentor. And while parents may try to build friendly connections, keeping things professional will help you navigate the ups and downs of teaching without getting your heart broken.

By maintaining these boundaries, you can create a more positive, productive, and fulfilling teaching experience for yourself, your students, and their families. Your professionalism sets the standard, and when you lead with integrity, your students and their parents will follow.

Chapter 9

Considering Studio Ownership

Have you ever dreamed of owning your own dance studio? For many dance teachers, the idea of opening their own studio is a natural progression in their career. It can be exciting to imagine a space where you set the rules, choose the curriculum, and build a dance community on your own terms. However, studio ownership is about much more than teaching dance. It's about running a business, and the day-to-day responsibilities can be very different from what many dance teachers imagine.

In this chapter, we'll explore the realities of studio ownership, from legal requirements and financial management to customer service and marketing. We'll also discuss the key differences between teaching dance and running a business, so you can decide if studio ownership is the right step for you.

Owning a dance studio can be incredibly rewarding, but it's also a serious commitment that requires a wide range of skills beyond dance teaching. While you might picture yourself creating choreography, mentoring students, and producing recitals, the truth is that much of your time as a studio owner will be spent on administrative tasks, financial planning, and managing people.

If your passion is teaching, impacting dancers, and creating beautiful choreography, then studio ownership might not be the best path for you. Instead, look for a home studio where you can have autonomy and leadership opportunities, where you can focus on teaching and building your dance legacy. On the other hand, if you find fulfillment in administration, marketing, managing people, having difficult conversations, crunching numbers, and customer service, then owning a dance studio could be a great fit.

Owning a studio means:

- Keeping track of finances, paying bills, and managing budgets.
- Handling marketing, social media, and customer outreach.
- Hiring, training, and sometimes letting go of staff.
- Dealing with customer complaints and ensuring a positive customer experience.
- Understanding and complying with legal requirements and labor laws.
- Developing policies, handling contracts, and ensuring your business is legally protected.

While there are aspects of studio ownership that are connected to dance, such as planning recitals, creating programs, and managing classes, the majority of your time will be spent on tasks that are necessary to keep the business running smoothly.

Before you can open your doors, there are several legal steps you'll need to take to ensure your studio is compliant with local, state, and federal regulations. Understanding the legal aspects of business ownership is crucial to avoid issues down the line.

When starting your dance studio, one of the first key decisions is determining the appropriate business structure. This choice will shape your responsibilities, liabilities, and tax obligations. For many new studio owners, a sole proprietorship may seem like the simplest option, as it makes you the sole owner responsible for all aspects of the business, including any debts or liabilities. However, for those seeking to protect personal assets, a Limited Liability Company (LLC) offers flexibility, shielding your personal property from business liabilities. This is a popular option for small businesses, as it combines legal protection with the freedom to run the studio as you see fit. If you're planning a larger studio or anticipate significant expansion, a corporation might be the best fit, though it comes with more complexity in terms of taxation and legal obligations. Consulting with a legal or financial professional can help you determine which structure aligns best with your goals.

Once you've selected your business structure, it's crucial to ensure you have all the necessary licenses and permits to operate legally. Depending on your location, this might include obtaining a general business license, health permits, or zoning permits. Researching local requirements will save you time and prevent potential legal issues down the road.

Another critical aspect of studio ownership is investing in the right insurance to protect your business. General liability insurance covers accidents or injuries on your premises, while professional liability insurance offers protection from claims related to your teaching services. If you have employees, workers' compensation insurance is required to cover medical expenses and lost wages in the event of an injury. Additionally, property insurance will protect the physical assets of your studio, such as equipment and the building itself.

Having contracts in place is another essential step in protecting your business. Clear agreements with employees, students, and vendors will outline expectations and reduce the likelihood of disputes. Employee contracts should cover pay, job responsibilities, and confidentiality, while student registration and tuition agreements ensure that parents understand the studio's policies. Vendor contracts are equally important, securing services such as cleaning or equipment maintenance.

One of the most critical aspects of running a dance studio is understanding financial management. While teaching may be your passion, keeping the business financially healthy is vital to its success. Creating a budget will give you a roadmap for covering both fixed and variable expenses like rent, utilities, salaries, and supplies. Knowing your numbers ensures that you can plan for future growth and avoid financial pitfalls.

A clear system for managing tuition and payments is also essential. Decide whether you'll charge monthly, quarterly, or by class and consider offering discounts for referrals or siblings. Many studios use software to automate billing and track payments, making the process easier for both you and the parents. Additionally, understanding your tax obligations as a business owner is more complex than when you're an employee. Keeping track of income, expenses, and payroll taxes is crucial, and hiring an accountant can help you navigate these complexities and ensure compliance.

As your studio grows, you may need to expand your space or hire more staff. Planning for growth by anticipating these changes will help you make informed financial decisions and ensure the studio's long-term success.

Of course, a successful studio isn't just about finances it's also about marketing and customer service. Even the best classes won't fill themselves if people don't know about them. Developing your brand and creating a consistent image that reflects your studio's mission is crucial. Are you focused on competitive dance, or do you prioritize community engagement and fun? Your website, social media presence, and marketing materials should reflect your brand's identity.

A marketing plan will help you outline strategies to attract new students and retain current ones. Social media platforms like Instagram and Facebook are great for showcasing your classes and engaging with potential students, while email newsletters keep parents informed about upcoming events and promotions. Offering referral programs or hosting community events can also help raise awareness of your studio.

At the heart of your studio's success is customer service. It's essential to create a welcoming, inclusive environment where students and parents feel valued. Being responsive to inquiries, addressing concerns promptly, and maintaining clear communication about classes and schedules are all crucial elements of excellent customer service.

Managing the people within your studio staff, students, and parents is another essential aspect of studio ownership. Hiring instructors who align with your studio's values and vision is important, as they are an extension of your brand. Look for teachers who are not only talented but also passionate educators. Providing clear job descriptions and regular feedback can help maintain a strong, cohesive team.

You'll also need to navigate difficult conversations, whether it's addressing conflicts with parents, handling disputes between students, or managing underperforming staff. These conversations require empathy, honesty, and a focus on finding solutions. Building a positive studio culture, where everyone feels respected and appreciated, will create an environment that fosters success. A strong, supportive culture will encourage higher retention rates and contribute to a happier, healthier community.

Is Studio Ownership Right for You?

Studio ownership is not for everyone, and that's okay. Running a dance studio is demanding, requiring skills that go beyond teaching dance. It involves balancing the roles of manager, marketer, financial planner, customer service representative, and, yes, sometimes dance teacher.

Ask Yourself These Questions:

1. Do you enjoy administrative tasks like scheduling, managing budgets, and handling paperwork?
2. Are you comfortable marketing your studio, building a brand, and dealing with social media?
3. Can you handle managing people, including having difficult conversations when needed?
4. Do you have a passion for customer service and making sure students and parents are happy?
5. Are you prepared to take on the financial risks and responsibilities of running a business?

If your passion lies in teaching and creating choreography, there are still many ways to build a successful and fulfilling career without owning a studio. Seek out studios that offer leadership opportunities, where you can develop your own programs or even take on roles that help guide the studio's direction. However, if you love the idea of building a business from the ground up, managing a team, and seeing the behind-the-scenes work that makes a studio thrive, then ownership could be a rewarding path for you.

Owning a dance studio can be an incredibly fulfilling experience, but it's not a decision to be taken lightly. It requires a diverse set of skills and a willingness to take on responsibilities that go far beyond teaching dance. The key to successful studio ownership is understanding that it's a business first and a dance space second.

If you're ready to embrace the challenges of marketing, financial management, customer service, and administration, owning a studio might be the perfect path for you. But if your heart lies in teaching, creating, and mentoring dancers, then find a studio that gives you the freedom and support to do what you love without the added stress of ownership.

No matter which path you choose, the dance industry needs passionate, dedicated professionals who want to make a difference. Whether you're leading from the studio floor or from behind the desk, your contribution can create a lasting impact on the dance community.

As a dance teacher, you have the opportunity to make a real impact on your students' lives, whether you choose to continue teaching or eventually open your own studio. This book provides you with the foundation, tools, and insights to thrive in your career, helping you turn your passion into a rewarding profession. Keep dancing, keep growing, and continue spreading the joy of dance.

Chapter 10

Self-Care and Preventing Burnout

No self-care can lead to stress. Over time, this stress can build up and lead to burnout, where you feel emotionally drained and disconnected from the work you once loved. The key to avoiding burnout is learning how to manage stress and set boundaries.

As a dance teacher, it can be easy to overextend yourself, saying yes to extra classes, private lessons, and responsibilities outside your normal teaching hours. While it's important to be flexible and accommodating, it's also essential to set boundaries to protect your time and energy. Being a dance teacher is one of the most rewarding professions, but it's also one of the most demanding. The role requires you to be physically active, emotionally present, and constantly creative. You give your energy, time, and passion to your students, often putting their needs before your own. While this dedication is admirable, it can also lead to burnout if you don't prioritize your own self-care. In this chapter, we'll explore the importance of maintaining your physical health, managing stress, and finding ways to recharge. By taking care of yourself, you'll be able to sustain your energy, enthusiasm, and love for teaching, even during tough times.

As a dance teacher, your body is your most valuable tool. You need it to demonstrate steps, guide students, and keep up with the demands of the classroom. That's why taking care of your physical health should be a top priority. Self-care isn't just about pampering yourself; it's about maintaining the physical strength and endurance you need to do your job effectively.

One of the most common issues dance teachers face is the risk of injury. Constantly demonstrating movements, correcting students, and being on your feet for long periods can take a toll on your body. Incorporating a regular stretching routine can help you stay flexible, prevent injuries, and reduce muscle tension.

To prevent injuries and maintain longevity as a dance teacher, it's important to prioritize certain practices. Always begin your classes with a proper warm-up. Just like your students, you need to prepare your body for physical activity by gently stretching and going through basic movements to activate your muscles. Listening to your body is essential. If you feel any discomfort or pain, don't push through it; pain is a signal that something may be wrong. Ignoring it could lead to more serious injuries. Taking breaks and seeking professional help when needed is crucial for long-term health. Cross-training through strength training, Pilates, yoga, or swimming can also benefit your body by improving muscle strength and flexibility while helping prevent overuse injuries. Finally, ensure you're incorporating rest and recovery into your schedule. Allowing your body to recover is just as important as the training itself, as it gives your muscles time to repair and grow stronger.

In addition to injury prevention, maintaining a healthy lifestyle is key to keeping your energy levels high and your body strong. A balanced diet rich in fruits, vegetables, lean proteins, and whole grains will provide the sustained energy you need throughout the day. Try to avoid relying on quick fixes like caffeine or sugary snacks, as these can lead to energy crashes later on. Hydration is another essential aspect. Teaching dance is physically demanding, and it's easy to become dehydrated while moving all day. Keep water handy during your classes and take frequent sips to stay hydrated. Getting enough sleep at least 7-8 hours per night is also critical for your physical and mental health. Sleep allows your body to recover and ensures you're mentally sharp for teaching. Finally, don't forget to schedule regular check-ups with a healthcare provider to stay on top of any health issues. Prioritizing your health ensures that you can teach effectively and continue doing what you love.

Taking care of yourself physically is essential to maintaining the energy and stamina required for teaching dance, but your emotional well-being is just as important. As a dance teacher, you're not only managing the physical demands of the classroom but also the emotional energy that comes with guiding students, navigating expectations, and dealing with the challenges of studio life. Emotional self-care involves recognizing the mental and emotional toll that teaching can take and finding ways to stay balanced, positive, and resilient. Just as you prioritize rest days for your body, it's crucial to build habits that support your emotional health to ensure you can continue to teach with passion and enthusiasm. Let's explore ways to take care of yourself emotionally and avoid burnout.

Dance teaching is not only physically demanding but also emotionally taxing. You invest a lot of yourself in your students, and the pressure to be constantly creative, energetic, and supportive

It's okay to say no to extra work if it means preserving your well-being. Politely but firmly decline requests that will overburden your schedule or add unnecessary stress. Prioritize the commitments that matter most and align with your goals.

Make sure your studio knows your availability and respects it. If you've agreed to work a certain number of hours, don't feel obligated to take on more unless you genuinely want to. Having a clear schedule helps you manage your time and reduces the risk of burnout.

Setting boundaries around communication is important for maintaining your personal time. Let students and parents know when you are available to answer questions and when you need to focus on your own downtime.

After prioritizing your emotional well-being, the next step in maintaining balance as a dance teacher is being proactive with time management. Emotional health and self-care are crucial, but managing your time effectively helps prevent stress from creeping in and ensures that you're staying on top of both your personal and professional responsibilities.

Juggling class preparation, student communication, administrative tasks, and your own downtime can be overwhelming without a solid plan. By organizing your time efficiently, you can create a sustainable routine that supports both your well-being and the success of your teaching. Let's explore strategies for managing your time and keeping everything in balance.

Effective time management can help you balance your teaching responsibilities with your personal life. By organizing your schedule, you can reduce stress and ensure that you're not constantly rushing from one task to another.

Take time at the beginning of each week to plan your classes, schedule meetings, and organize your personal time. Knowing what to expect will help you feel more in control. I highly recommend taking an hour on Sunday to plan out your week. Make a "Brain Dump" list of all things you need and want to accomplish. Once your Brain Dump is done section your list into columns that make sense for your life, Teaching, Admin, Relationship, House Chores, whatever makes sense for you. Access the list and prioritize, maybe you can move some less important items to next week's list. Maybe there are some items on your list you can delegate to someone else, or you can assess whether or not an item truly is needed based on your time and other priorities. Once you have your prioritized list plug those items into a calendar and set the day and time you will do those tasks.

Pro- Tip: While doing your Sunday Brain Dump plan out your meals and do some meal prepping. Not having to think about food will free up your brain for more creative things!

Enter your week confidently by including lesson planning in your Sunday Planning. Preparing your lessons in advance can save you time and stress during the week. It also allows you to plan engaging and well-structured classes without feeling rushed.

After planning your week and structuring your responsibilities, the next step is ensuring that you create space for a personal life alongside your teaching career. While having a clear plan helps you stay organized and focused in the studio, it's equally important to carve out time for yourself, family, and friends. Teaching dance can be all-consuming, but finding balance between your work and personal life is key to avoiding burnout and maintaining long-term happiness. By prioritizing self-care and setting boundaries around your personal time, you can foster a healthy, sustainable lifestyle both inside and outside the studio.

When you're passionate about teaching, it's easy to let your work consume your life. Just as you schedule classes and meetings, schedule time for yourself. Whether it's an hour to read, go for a walk, or spend time with loved ones, make sure you're giving yourself moments to unwind and recharge.

Explore hobbies or activities that are unrelated to dance. This could be painting, cooking, hiking, or learning a new skill. Having interests outside of your teaching career can give you a sense of fulfillment and help you avoid burnout.

If you're feeling overwhelmed, don't hesitate to reach out for support. Talk to your colleagues, studio management, or friends and family. Sometimes, simply sharing your concerns can lighten the load, and they may have helpful advice or solutions.

Finding balance between your teaching responsibilities and personal life is essential to maintaining your well-being, but it's also important to ensure that you're taking time to recharge and stay passionate about teaching. While a balanced routine helps keep stress at bay, recharging allows you to reconnect with the reasons you became a dance teacher in the first place. Whether it's through attending workshops, exploring new creative outlets, or simply taking time away from the studio, finding ways to reignite your passion will help you bring fresh energy into your classes and continue to inspire your students. Let's dive into strategies for recharging and maintaining enthusiasm for your teaching career.

Even the most passionate dance teachers can experience periods of diminished motivation or inspiration. Constantly giving your energy to students and focusing on their growth can leave you feeling drained. It's essential to find ways to recharge and reconnect with your own love for dance to maintain your enthusiasm over the long term. Taking the time to nurture your personal connection to dance can reignite your passion and remind you why you chose this path in the first place.

One of the best ways to recharge is to step back into the role of a student. Attending a class for yourself allows you to learn new skills, explore different styles, and experience the joy of dancing without the pressure of teaching. This shift in perspective can refresh your outlook and inspire new ideas for your own classes. Similarly, choreographing just for fun without the need to create a polished performance lets you experiment creatively, reigniting the artistic side of your dance practice.

Watching others perform can also be a great source of inspiration. Whether you attend live performances, watch online videos, or revisit your favorite dance films, observing how other dancers express themselves can remind you of the beauty and power of dance. These moments can reignite the same passion that first drew you to teaching.

Continued learning is another way to stay motivated and bring fresh energy to your teaching. Attending workshops, conferences, or conventions gives you the opportunity to engage with the broader dance community, learn from other professionals, and gain new perspectives. Pursuing certifications in areas like acrobatics, flexibility training, or teaching special populations can also open up new opportunities and keep your skills sharp, which in turn fuels your passion. Additionally, reading books and articles on dance education can keep you informed and provide fresh ideas to incorporate into your lessons.

Lastly, teaching dance requires emotional as well as physical energy. It's crucial to invest in your own mental and emotional well-being. Supporting your students, celebrating their successes, and guiding them through challenges can be emotionally demanding, so making time for self-care ensures you can continue giving your best to your students while staying passionate and fulfilled in your own dance journey.

Taking just a few minutes each day to clear your mind can help you manage stress, improve focus, and maintain a sense of calm. Mindfulness practices can also help you stay grounded and present in the moment. Writing about your experiences as a teacher can be a great way to process your emotions and reflect on what you've accomplished. It can also help you recognize patterns of stress and find ways to address them. If you're struggling with feelings of stress, anxiety, or burnout, consider seeking support from a mental health professional. There's no shame in asking for help, and sometimes talking to someone outside of your immediate circle can provide valuable insights.

Being a dance teacher is an incredibly special role, but it's also one that requires a lot of energy, patience, and resilience. To be the best teacher you can be, you need to take care of yourself first. Self-care isn't selfish it's a necessary part of being able to give your best to your students. When you're physically healthy, mentally strong, and emotionally balanced, you can show up for your students with the passion, creativity, and dedication that makes dance education so meaningful.

Remember that it's okay to prioritize your own well-being. By setting boundaries, managing stress, and finding ways to recharge, you're not only taking care of yourself but also setting an example for your students. You're showing them the importance of balance, self-respect, and the ability to sustain their passions over the long term.

Teaching dance is a marathon, not a sprint. There will be days when you're tired, uninspired, or overwhelmed, but there will also be days of pure joy and fulfillment. By embracing self-care, you can navigate the ups and downs with grace, continue to grow as a teacher, and keep sharing your love of dance with others for many years to come.

Chapter 11

Effective Communication

Effective communication is a cornerstone of successful teaching, especially in dance where feedback, guidance, and relationship-building are critical to students' development. How you communicate whether with your students, their parents, or your fellow instructors can influence the dynamics of your classes and the overall studio environment. Communication goes beyond words; it includes how you convey your thoughts, how you listen to others, and the non-verbal cues you use to reinforce your message. In this chapter, we'll explore the importance of constructive communication, strategies for handling challenging conversations, and the impact of non-verbal communication in the dance classroom.

Giving feedback to students is one of the most crucial elements of effective dance instruction. The way feedback is delivered can either motivate or demoralize students. Poorly communicated feedback can make students feel discouraged or inadequate, while positive, actionable feedback can help them grow, both technically and emotionally. Constructive feedback must be specific, actionable, and encouraging. For example, instead of saying, "Good job," you might say, "I loved how you extended your arm in that movement, but try to lift your chin a little higher to enhance your posture." This type of feedback helps students understand exactly what they did well and where they can improve, without feeling criticized.

It's also important to focus on a student's effort and progress rather than just the result. Acknowledging hard work, even when a student hasn't fully mastered a skill, encourages persistence and resilience. For instance, saying, "I can see you've been practicing your turns, and your balance has improved so much. Keep working on spotting, and you'll nail that double pirouette," provides positive reinforcement while directing the student toward continued growth. The "sandwich method" of feedback, where you offer constructive criticism between two positive comments, is another effective strategy. This approach softens the feedback, making students more receptive to it, and studies suggest younger generations of dancers respond especially well to high levels of positive reinforcement.

In addition to verbal feedback, non-verbal communication plays a significant role in dance instruction. Your tone, facial expressions, and body language can reinforce or contradict what you say. A calm, supportive tone will motivate students to keep trying, while a harsh or impatient tone may cause them to feel anxious or afraid to make mistakes. Being mindful of how you deliver feedback is crucial to creating a nurturing learning environment.

Another powerful way to engage students is by encouraging self-reflection. Asking questions like, "How did that turn feel?" or "What do you think you could do to make that movement smoother?" prompts students to evaluate their own performance. This not only fosters self-awareness but also helps students develop the ability to self-correct, an essential skill for any dancer aiming to improve.

While managing communication with students is crucial, dance teachers must also navigate communication with parents, which can sometimes be more challenging. Parents are often heavily invested in their child's success, and their expectations may not always align with the realities of the studio's curriculum or their child's progress. Setting clear expectations from the beginning is key to avoiding misunderstandings. Whether it's through an introductory email at the start of the term, a parent meeting, or a detailed class syllabus, making sure parents understand your goals, policies, and communication methods upfront will help prevent conflicts down the road.

When difficult conversations with parents do arise whether it's about a student's behavior, their progress, or a sensitive topic like class placement it's essential to approach these discussions with professionalism and empathy. Preparing for the conversation in advance will help ensure that your message is clear and respectful. Starting with a positive comment about the student, being honest yet empathetic, and focusing on finding solutions together will make these conversations more productive. For instance, rather than saying, "Sarah is always disruptive in class," you could say, "I've noticed that Sarah seems distracted during class, and I'm concerned it's affecting her progress." This reframes the issue in a way that invites collaboration rather than conflict.

Managing expectations is another vital part of communicating with parents. Be transparent about the objectives of each class, and remind parents that every student progresses at their own pace. By clearly outlining class placement policies and performance expectations, you help manage parental expectations and reduce potential disappointment. Additionally, encourage open communication with parents, while also setting clear boundaries to protect your time. Let parents know how and when they can contact you for non-urgent questions, such as through email rather than impromptu discussions right after class.

By focusing on clear, constructive communication and establishing professional boundaries, you can create a healthy, respectful learning environment that benefits both your students and their families. Through effective communication, you can foster trust and mutual respect, ensuring that your students thrive both technically and personally while maintaining positive relationships with their parents.

Non-Verbal Communication in Dance Teaching

In dance, non-verbal communication is just as important as verbal communication, if not more so. Dance is, after all, a physical art form, and many of the corrections and instructions you give will be demonstrated rather than spoken. Being mindful of your body language, facial expressions, and physical cues can help you convey your message clearly and effectively.

Demonstrating corrections is a fundamental part of teaching dance. When students can see what you're asking them to do, it helps them understand the movement on a deeper level. For example:

Mirroring: Stand facing your students and mirror the movements you want them to perform. This allows them to see the correct posture, alignment, and dynamics.

Highlighting Specific Movements: If you're correcting a specific part of a movement, use your hands or body to draw attention to that area. For example, if a student's arm placement is off, you can gently guide their arm to the correct position, showing them the adjustment without needing to explain it verbally.

Demonstrating Effort and Energy: Use your own body language to emphasize the energy, fluidity, or strength you want your students to express. Show them how to stretch their arms fully or engage their core, and they'll be able to replicate that feeling in their own movements.

Your facial expressions can have a big impact on how your students feel during class. A smile, a nod, or a look of encouragement can boost a student's confidence and let them know they're on the right track. Conversely, a look of frustration or impatience can make a student feel anxious and self-conscious. Being mindful of your facial expressions ensures that you're conveying positivity and support.

Eye contact is a powerful tool for communication. It helps build connection, conveys sincerity, and shows that you are engaged and paying attention. When giving instructions, corrections, or feedback, make sure to make eye contact with your students. This lets them know you are focused on them and that they have your full attention.

In dance teaching, physical touch can be necessary to help students understand positioning and alignment. However, it's important to be mindful of how and when you use physical touch, especially with younger students or those who might be uncomfortable with it. Always ask for consent before physically adjusting a student, and be respectful of their personal space.

Best Practices for Using Physical Touch in Class:

Ask for Permission: Always ask before you make a physical adjustment. For example, "Is it okay if I adjust your arm position?" This simple question shows respect for the student's boundaries and ensures they are comfortable.

Explain What You're Doing: When making an adjustment, explain what you're doing and why. This helps the student understand the purpose of the correction and learn how to make the adjustment themselves in the future.

Use Visual Demonstrations First: Before resorting to physical touch, try demonstrating the movement yourself or using a visual aid. This can often help students understand the correction without needing physical adjustment.

Effective communication isn't just about talking; it's also about listening. Being a good listener helps you build stronger relationships with your students and their parents, and it allows you to understand their needs, concerns, and feelings.

Listening to your students shows that you respect their opinions and care about their progress. It also gives you valuable insights into how they're experiencing your class, what they're struggling with, and what they enjoy. Create a space where students feel comfortable sharing their thoughts, and take the time to listen when they do.

When speaking with parents, practice active listening. This means giving them your full attention, acknowledging their concerns, and responding thoughtfully. Even if you don't agree with everything a parent says, showing that you're willing to listen can go a long way in building trust and resolving conflicts.

Tips for Active Listening:

Maintain Eye Contact: This shows the speaker that you are engaged and interested in what they're saying.

Nod and Provide Verbal Acknowledgements: Simple responses like "I see" or "I understand" let the speaker know that you're following along.

Paraphrase and Reflect: After the speaker finishes, paraphrase what they said to confirm your understanding. For example, "So, you're concerned that Sarah isn't getting enough individual attention in class. Is that right?"

Avoid Interrupting: Let the speaker finish before you respond. Interrupting can make them feel like their opinions aren't valued.

Effective communication is one of the most powerful tools you have as a dance teacher. Whether you're giving feedback to students, speaking with parents, or demonstrating movements through non-verbal cues, the way you communicate can make or break your effectiveness as an educator. By being clear, empathetic, and respectful in your communication, you can build a classroom environment that fosters trust, respect, and growth.

Remember, every interaction you have whether with a student, a parent, or a colleague is an opportunity to build a positive connection. Approach each conversation with patience, understanding, and a genuine desire to help, and you'll create a teaching environment where everyone feels heard, supported, and inspired.

Chapter 12

Inclusivity and Accessibility in Dance

The world of dance has long been admired for its beauty, grace, and ability to convey emotion. However, it has also faced criticism for its exclusivity, particularly regarding who is considered to have the "right" body type, background, or level of ability to participate. As the dance industry evolves, inclusivity and accessibility are becoming increasingly important, reflecting a broader shift toward celebrating diversity and ensuring that everyone has the opportunity to experience the joy of dance.

In this chapter, we will explore how to create an inclusive environment that welcomes students of all backgrounds, abilities, and body types. We will also provide strategies for teaching students with different learning needs or physical disabilities, and discuss ways to promote body positivity, helping to foster a culture where all dancers feel valued and supported, regardless of their skill level or physique.

Inclusivity means making sure that every student feels welcome, respected, and able to participate fully, regardless of their background, physical appearance, or skill level. An inclusive environment is one where students of different races, ethnicities, body types, gender identities, and abilities can feel safe and supported. This starts with the way the dance studio is run, the language teachers use, and the attitudes and policies set by studio management.

An inclusive dance class begins with setting a culture of respect and acceptance. Every student should feel that they belong, and this can only happen when teachers, students, and staff are committed to creating a welcoming environment.

Be mindful of the words you use. Avoid terms that might be exclusive or discriminatory, and choose language that is neutral, respectful, and encouraging. For example, rather than saying "girls" or "boys" in class, consider using "dancers" or "everyone." Address students by their preferred names and pronouns, and make it clear that your class is a safe space for all gender identities.

Recognize and celebrate the diversity of your students, whether it's through showcasing different cultural dance styles, encouraging self-expression, or acknowledging the unique strengths each dancer brings to the studio. This can help students feel seen and appreciated for who they are.

Make sure your students understand that your class is a place where kindness and respect are mandatory. Address any bullying, teasing, or exclusionary behavior immediately and set clear consequences for those actions. Creating an atmosphere of mutual respect will make your class a safer and more welcoming place for all dancers.

As a dance teacher, you set the tone for your classroom. Demonstrate inclusivity through your actions, words, and attitude. Be approachable, open-minded, and willing to learn about the needs and perspectives of your students.

Every student learns differently, and it's important to recognize and accommodate those differences in your teaching. Some students may have physical disabilities, learning disabilities, or neurodiverse conditions like ADHD or autism. With the right strategies, you can make dance accessible and enjoyable for students of all abilities.

I am not an expert in teaching dancers with disabilities. I truly believe this is such an important job to do well and it is out of my educational scope. I can, however, recommend the Rhythm Works program. I have taken workshops from Tricia Garcia and I can wholeheartedly recommend any of her programs. I actually recommend her Rhythm Works program even if you aren't teaching dancers who have a disability. Learning how the brain works only makes you a better teacher and so many kids are on a spectrum of neurodivergence.

Promoting Body Positivity in Dance

This is definitely something I can speak on! I grew up being the biggest dancer in the room. I know what it's like to feel like you don't "fit" in a dance class. Being an advocate for self-confidence and body positivity I wrote a children's book called Bella Bunny. Bella Bunny is set in the dance studio and Bella learns how to love the fur she is in, stand up to bullies and find the confidence to shine on stage.

Why did I choose to write a book about body positivity? Well, the dance world has long been plagued by unrealistic body standards that can lead to feelings of inadequacy, low self-esteem, and even disordered eating among dancers. Promoting body positivity and fostering a culture of acceptance is essential to creating a healthier, more inclusive dance environment.

Body positivity is about embracing and celebrating all body types, acknowledging that there is no single "ideal" dancer's body. Every body is capable of expressing beauty, grace, and strength, and the dance studio should be a place where all dancers feel confident and empowered. Encourage your students to appreciate their bodies for their abilities, not their appearance. Celebrate strength, flexibility, and creativity. For example, instead of praising a dancer for having "long legs," praise their strong turnout or ability to execute a clean pirouette. Be mindful of the language you use when talking about the body. Avoid making comments about weight, size, or appearance, even if they seem complimentary. Focus on functional, positive language, such as "strong," "powerful," or "graceful." Allow your students to express their individuality through dance. Every dancer has their own unique style and personality, and this should be celebrated. Encourage students to find joy in how their body moves, rather than striving to fit a narrow standard. Promote a balanced, healthy approach to fitness and self-care. This includes emphasizing the importance of proper nutrition, hydration, rest, and mental health. Encourage your students to take care of themselves and listen to their bodies, and be sure to model this behavior as a teacher.

If you notice that a student is struggling with body image issues, it's important to handle the situation with sensitivity and care. Make it clear that your studio is a place of acceptance and that all dancers are valued for who they are, not what they look like. If a student expresses concerns about their body, listen without judgment and offer support. In some cases, it may be appropriate to alert a parent so the dancer can get professional medical support.

Creating an inclusive, accessible, and body-positive dance environment is not just the right thing to do; it also brings numerous benefits to your class and your studio. When students of different backgrounds, abilities, and body types come together, they bring unique perspectives, experiences, and strengths. This diversity enriches the learning environment, encouraging creativity, collaboration, and empathy. It helps students see dance as a universal language that can be expressed in countless ways.

Inclusive teaching helps students feel valued and supported. When students see that they are welcome, regardless of their body type, ability, or background, it boosts their self-esteem and encourages them to take risks, express themselves, and push their limits. An inclusive environment is one where all students can grow and thrive.

Inclusivity helps build a stronger, more connected dance community. When students learn to accept and support each other, they carry those values outside of the studio and into the wider world. Dance becomes a tool for promoting empathy, understanding, and unity.

Inclusivity and accessibility in dance are not just about making accommodations they are about fundamentally reshaping how we view dance education. By creating a space where all dancers, regardless of their background, body type, or ability, feel welcomed and valued, we can foster a more diverse, creative, and supportive dance community.

As a dance teacher, you have the power to lead this change. You can model inclusivity, adapt your teaching methods, and promote body positivity, helping your students see that dance is not about fitting a certain mold but about expressing themselves in a way that is true and beautiful. Dance has the power to bring people together, and by making your class inclusive and accessible, you're helping to share that power with everyone.

Remember, dance is for everyone. It's for the little girl who dreams of pirouetting across the stage, the boy who wants to express himself through movement, the teenager who finds confidence in choreography, and the person who has always been told their body doesn't fit the mold. Dance is for all of them—and by championing inclusivity and accessibility, you're making sure they all have a place to dance.

Chapter 13

Leadership positions inside a dance studio and how to promote

Being part of a dance studio that offers leadership opportunities is essential for career growth and long-term job satisfaction. As a dance teacher, the ability to advance your career within a studio not only helps you develop professionally but also strengthens your ties to the community and the studio itself. A studio that provides pathways for leadership roles allows teachers to take on greater responsibility, showcase their skills beyond the classroom, and contribute meaningfully to the studio's overall mission and success.

Career advancement within a dance studio is highly achievable through leadership positions, which can range from administrative roles to program development. Teachers who demonstrate initiative and the desire to contribute to the studio's growth can take on leadership roles that align with their strengths and passions. Whether it's running a new program, spearheading community performances, or assisting with day-to-day operations, these roles can help teachers expand their influence and create lasting impact both in and outside the studio.

Leadership positions in a dance studio can vary widely depending on the needs of the business. Some common roles include program directors, camp coordinators, community outreach leaders, or administrative managers. Teachers can also take on specific projects such as organizing events, creating new class offerings, or managing competitive teams. These positions not only foster personal growth but also ensure the studio thrives as a dynamic, well-managed organization.

When it comes to advancing your career as a dance teacher, leadership roles within a studio offer the perfect opportunity to grow professionally while making a meaningful impact on both students and the studio as a whole. These positions allow teachers to step into roles that go beyond teaching, enabling them to contribute to the development of programs, foster community engagement, and support the studio's administrative and operational needs. By taking on leadership responsibilities, teachers can shape the direction of the studio, enrich the student experience, and gain valuable management skills that enhance their career trajectory.

Now, let's explore some of the leadership roles that could be available in a studio setting, offering exciting opportunities for career advancement. These roles allow teachers to take initiative, expand their influence, and help the studio thrive in new and dynamic ways.

1. Start a New Program the Studio Does Not Offer: Taking the initiative to introduce a new program that the studio currently doesn't offer can position you as

a leader in innovation. Whether it's introducing a genre like acro, hip-hop, or ballroom, or starting a program like dance fitness or adaptive dance for students with dissabilities, creating something new fills a gap in the studio's offerings and broadens its appeal. This allows you to showcase your creativity, foresight, and ability to meet market demands. It also demonstrates your dedication to the studio's growth, and can help attract new students while retaining current ones.

2. Plan Community Performances: Organizing community performances is a great way to boost the studio's visibility while also demonstrating your leadership skills. By arranging for students to perform at local events, festivals, or charity functions, you create an opportunity for dancers to showcase their talent outside of the studio, contributing to their confidence and experience. These performances also strengthen the studio's relationship with the local community, drawing in potential new students and fostering goodwill. Spearheading such projects demonstrates your initiative and ability to manage events, as well as your commitment to using dance as a positive force in the community.

3. Start or Run a Day Camp During Times the Studio is Closed: Running a day camp during school holidays or studio off-weeks not only helps fill the gaps when regular classes aren't in session but also

allows you to offer something exciting to the student body. These camps can be focused on various themes intensives, choreography boot camps, or fun creative camps for younger students. Camps can generate additional income for the studio while also providing students with extra training opportunities. Taking the lead on these types of projects shows your ability to plan and manage extracurricular activities that benefit both the students and the studio.

4. Offer Birthday Parties: Dance-themed birthday parties are a fun and creative service you can offer, which helps engage the local community while also promoting the studio. By planning and hosting themed birthday parties, you allow young students and their friends to experience the fun of dance in a celebratory atmosphere. This is also an excellent way to attract new families to the studio who might not have been exposed to dance classes otherwise. Running birthday parties demonstrates your ability to think outside the box to create revenue-generating opportunities and attract new clientele while making the studio a community hub.

5. Ask to Help with Admin Projects: Stepping up to assist with administrative tasks or projects is a great way to showcase your leadership skills and initiative beyond the classroom. Whether it's helping with scheduling, registration, or studio marketing efforts, assisting with admin work gives you a deeper

understanding of how the studio operates. By stepping in to handle these important behind-the-scenes tasks, you not only relieve some of the burden from the studio owner but also demonstrate your dedication to the studio's overall success. This involvement can lead to more leadership responsibilities and a deeper integration into the management side of the business.

Chapter 14

Building a Personal Brand as a Dance Teacher

In today's digital age, building a personal brand is more important than ever. For dance teachers looking to grow their careers, a strong personal brand can be a powerful tool that helps you stand out, connect with a wider community, and open up new opportunities. Whether you're seeking to teach at multiple studios, attract students for private lessons, or establish yourself as an expert in the dance community, your personal brand is a way to showcase who you are, what you stand for, and what makes your teaching unique.

This chapter will guide you through the process of defining your personal brand, using social media and online platforms to promote your work, and leveraging your brand to grow your career in new and exciting ways.

The foundation of any personal brand is a clear understanding of who you are and what you offer. As a dance teacher, this means defining your unique teaching style, your values, and what sets you apart from others. Your personal brand should reflect your passion for dance, your approach to teaching, and the impact you want to have on your students.

Every dance teacher has a distinct way of teaching. Some may focus on technique and discipline, while others emphasize creativity and self-expression. To define your teaching style, ask yourself the following questions:

What are my core teaching values?

Think about what matters most to you as a teacher. Are you focused on building strong technical skills, fostering creativity, or nurturing confidence and self-esteem in your students? Your core values will be the guiding principles of your brand and will influence everything from the way you teach to how you communicate with your audience.

How do I approach teaching?

Consider your approach in the classroom. Are you known for your patience and encouragement, or are you a high-energy teacher who pushes students to excel? Do you use humor and playfulness to make learning fun, or are you more structured and focused on discipline? Understanding your approach will help you communicate your style to potential students, parents, and collaborators.

What makes my classes unique?

Think about the elements that make your classes stand out. Do you incorporate creative exercises that encourage improvisation? Do you have a special way of teaching certain techniques that helps students grasp them more easily? Highlighting these unique aspects can help differentiate your brand from others.

What do I want students to remember about my classes? Reflect on the impact you want to have on your students. When they leave your class, how do you want them to feel? What lessons do you hope they take away? This can help you identify the core message of your brand.

Developing a Personal Teaching Philosophy

Once you've reflected on your teaching style, values, and goals, it's time to put it all together into a personal teaching philosophy. This is a statement that encapsulates your approach to teaching and what you aim to achieve as a dance educator. Your teaching philosophy can be used on your website, social media profiles, and promotional materials to give people a clear sense of who you are and what you stand for.

Example of a Teaching Philosophy

As a dance teacher, my goal is to create a supportive and inclusive environment where students can build confidence, develop technical skills, and express themselves through movement. I believe that every student has the potential to grow, and I strive to provide guidance that helps them reach their full potential while celebrating their individuality.

Now that you have established who you are as a teacher, your values, and what makes you unique it's time to tell the world. Social media and personal websites are essential tools for building your personal brand as a dance teacher. They allow you to share your journey, connect with a broader community, and showcase your skills, achievements, and unique teaching style. When used effectively, these platforms can help you expand your reach, attract new students, and build a loyal following.

In today's digital age, building a personal brand as a dance teacher is essential for growth and success. While passion and skill are foundational to any dance career, how you present yourself to the world, share your journey, and engage with others plays an increasingly important role in opening doors to new opportunities. With the vast number of platforms available, it's crucial to know where to focus your energy and how to leverage each platform's strengths. Social media and personal websites have become indispensable tools for dance teachers to expand their reach and connect with their community.

With so many social media platforms at your fingertips, it can feel overwhelming to figure out which ones will work best for you as a dance teacher. Each platform serves a different purpose and attracts a unique audience, so understanding how to harness the power of each is key to promoting your work effectively.

Instagram stands out as one of the most popular platforms for dance teachers, and it's no surprise why. Dance is a visual art, and Instagram offers a perfect medium for sharing that visual beauty. Whether you're posting photos of your classes, videos of your choreography, or behind-the-scenes moments from rehearsals, Instagram allows you to capture and share the essence of your teaching. Instagram Stories and Reels are particularly useful for quick tips, tutorials, or fun dance challenges, giving your audience bite-sized pieces of content that they can engage with instantly. You can also build a rapport with your audience by responding to comments and direct messages, keeping the conversation going beyond just the posts themselves.

For those looking to build a sense of community around their personal brand, Facebook is a great platform. It offers more than just a place to post updates; it's where you can foster deeper connections with your audience. By creating a Facebook Page dedicated to your work, you can share events, educational content, and updates about your classes. But the real magic often happens in Facebook Groups. Starting a group for your students or followers allows them to ask questions, share their progress, and build relationships with one another. This type of engagement goes a long way toward creating loyalty and a feeling of belonging.

For teachers who enjoy creating in-depth educational content, YouTube is an invaluable platform. With its focus on video content, YouTube is ideal for sharing longer-form tutorials, choreography breakdowns, and instructional videos. Over time, you can build a library of content that not only helps students learn but also showcases your teaching style and expertise. If you're interested in establishing yourself as a knowledgeable resource in the dance community, creating valuable, educational videos on YouTube can attract a wide audience of dancers eager to learn from you.

TikTok is all about quick, engaging videos and has become a powerhouse platform for creative and lighthearted content. For dance teachers, TikTok is perfect for sharing dance tips, fun choreography challenges, or keeping up with the latest dance trends. Its younger audience makes it a great tool for reaching teens and young adults who are passionate about dance. TikTok's fast-paced environment is also conducive to experimenting with new content and keeping things fresh.

Though LinkedIn might not seem like an obvious choice for a dance teacher, it's a platform that offers opportunities for professional networking. On LinkedIn, you can connect with studio owners, event organizers, and other dance professionals. Sharing your teaching experience, certifications, and achievements on this platform can help you build relationships with people who can offer you teaching opportunities, guest spots, or collaboration prospects. It's also a place where you can establish your professional presence in the broader arts education community.

While social media platforms allow you to connect with a wide audience, a personal website gives you a centralized space where you can present a professional, cohesive version of your brand. Your website acts as your virtual resume, portfolio, and point of contact. It's where potential students, studio owners, and collaborators can learn more about you and your offerings.

About Me Page

This is where you get to tell your story. Share your background, teaching philosophy, and experience in dance. Including a professional photo and a well-crafted bio adds a personal touch while highlighting your qualifications, certifications, and unique teaching approach. An engaging About Me page helps visitors connect with you on a personal level while understanding what sets you apart as a teacher.

Classes and Services

It's essential that your website clearly outlines what you offer whether it's group classes, private lessons, workshops, or online courses. Make sure to provide details about class levels, schedules, and how students can register. Transparency and accessibility are key here; potential students should be able to easily see what you offer and how to get involved.

Portfolio

A portfolio section on your website showcases your choreography, performance highlights, and any notable projects you've been part of. You can include videos, photos, and testimonials from students or collaborators to give a well-rounded view of your work. This is especially helpful when you're trying to attract new students or collaborators who want to see evidence of your skills and creativity.

Blog or Educational Content

Including a blog on your website allows you to share tips, insights, and advice related to dance. This not only helps you establish your expertise, but it also boosts your website's visibility through search engine optimization (SEO). By writing about your teaching methods, personal experiences, or industry trends, you can connect with readers on a deeper level while increasing the chances of new visitors finding your site.

Contact Information

Don't forget to make it easy for visitors to get in touch with you. Include a contact form or a clearly visible email address, along with links to your social media profiles. The more accessible you are, the more likely you are to attract inquiries about your services or collaborations.

You put the work in, you built out your social media and your website... now what? Building a personal brand is about more than showcasing your work; it's about forming meaningful connections with your audience. Engaging with followers on social media and your website fosters a sense of community, which leads to greater loyalty and support.

Respond to comments, ask questions, and create content that invites interaction. For example, you can create a poll asking your followers what dance-related topic they'd like you to cover next. The more you involve your audience in your content creation process, the more invested they'll feel in your journey.

Once your personal brand is established, it can serve as a springboard for new opportunities, from guest teaching and choreography commissions to developing your own curriculum. Here's how you can leverage your brand to grow your career in exciting new directions.

As your personal brand grows, you may be invited to guest teach at other studios, schools, or dance conventions. Guest teaching is an excellent way to expand your reach, share your expertise, and connect with new students.

To make the most of these opportunities, ensure you promote your availability on your website and social media profiles. Mention the types of workshops you offer and highlight past guest teaching engagements. Creating a workshop portfolio, including specific themes or techniques you specialize in, will help studio owners or event organizers understand how you can add value to their programs.

Networking is also crucial. Attending dance conventions or showcases where studio owners and event organizers are present can lead to new guest teaching opportunities. Building relationships with these professionals will open doors to teaching opportunities that align with your goals.

Another way to expand your career is through choreography commissions. By showcasing your best choreography on your website and social media, you can attract other studios, and more, that are looking for fresh pieces for their performances and competitions. Be sure to include your pricing on your website and the information on how to book you for choreography.

Offering your choreography as a service is a great way to expand your reach as a dance teacher, allowing you to share your creative vision with other studios, dance teams, and even special events. But, while choreography can be a powerful service offering, developing your own curriculum for sale is another opportunity to build a lasting impact in the industry. Creating a curriculum provides an in-depth, structured approach to teaching that can help other instructors improve their classes and ensure a consistent learning experience for their students. By turning your teaching methods into a well-rounded curriculum, you're offering something that goes beyond one-time choreography and establishes you as an authority in dance education. Both avenues offer unique ways to grow your personal brand and generate additional revenue while contributing meaningfully to the broader dance community.

If you have a distinct teaching approach, developing your own curriculum is another way to build your brand and create new opportunities. A well-structured curriculum not only sets you apart from other teachers but also positions you as an expert in a specific style or technique. This can open doors for you to teach at different studios, host workshops, or even publish educational materials.

To start, think about what you excel at as a teacher. Are you particularly good at helping beginners progress quickly? Do you have unique choreography exercises?

Use these strengths to build a curriculum that reflects your expertise. Once you have a structured guide, you can introduce it to other teachers through workshops or offer it as a downloadable resource, generating additional revenue streams.

As your brand grows, you may find opportunities to collaborate with relevant brands, such as dancewear companies or fitness organizations. These partnerships can help you reach new audiences, gain credibility, and form mutually beneficial relationships.

Start by identifying brands that align with your values and target audience. Reach out to them with collaboration proposals, whether it's for product sponsorships, affiliate marketing, or co-branded content. Collaborating with other dance influencers or teachers is another great way to expand your reach. Hosting joint events, creating collaborative videos, or cross-promoting each other's content can help you tap into each other's audiences and grow together.

Building a personal brand as a dance teacher isn't just about self-promotion; it's about sharing your passion, connecting with like-minded individuals, and creating a positive impact on your community. A strong brand reflects your teaching style, values, and personality, helping you attract opportunities that align with your goals.

By choosing the right social media platforms, creating a professional website, and engaging with your audience, you can cultivate a brand that resonates with students and colleagues alike. Whether you're teaching locally, guest teaching globally, or developing your own curriculum, your brand will serve as a beacon that highlights your dedication to the art of dance.

Stay authentic, be consistent, and continue to nurture your passion. As your personal brand grows, so will your opportunities to inspire, teach, and leave a lasting impact on the world of dance.

Chapter 15

Case Studies and Guest Contributions

One of the most inspiring aspects of being a dance teacher is the opportunity to learn from the experiences of others who have walked a similar path. Whether it's hearing how a fellow teacher built a thriving career, understanding what studio owners prioritize when hiring, or exploring the diverse career paths available within the dance industry, these real-life stories provide valuable insights and motivation. In this chapter, we'll feature case studies and guest contributions that showcase different journeys, highlight successes, and offer practical advice for dance teachers looking to grow their careers.

Case Study 1: Building a Multi-Faceted Career Sarah's Story

Sarah's journey as a dance teacher is a powerful example of how diversifying skills and seizing new opportunities can lead to a sustainable and rewarding career in dance education. After graduating from college with a degree in dance, Sarah began her career at a small local studio, eager to teach and share her passion. Like many new dance teachers, she initially focused on teaching basic technique classes, working with various age groups and styles. But she quickly realized that if she wanted to build a long-term, full-time career in the dance industry, she would need to expand her skill set and create a brand that could offer more to her students and the community.

In the first few years of her teaching career, Sarah felt both the excitement and challenges that come with working in a competitive field. She loved teaching, but she found that her schedule was inconsistent, and there were limitations on how many classes she could offer. During this time, she noticed how much the industry valued teachers who had multiple certifications or specialized in particular areas of dance. Sarah recognized that if she wanted to stand out and build a stable, multi-faceted career, she would need to invest in her professional development.

Sarah decided to start exploring additional certifications and educational opportunities. She attended workshops, teacher intensives, and professional development courses, all while continuing to teach her regular classes. She realized that by acquiring additional skills and broadening her knowledge, she could enhance her teaching and offer a wider variety of classes, ultimately increasing her value as an instructor.

One of the first steps Sarah took toward diversifying her career was earning certifications in areas beyond traditional dance styles. She became a certified Pilates instructor, which not only helped her improve her understanding of the body's mechanics but also gave her the ability to offer conditioning classes for dancers. These classes were a hit with both students and parents, as they focused on strength, flexibility, and injury prevention skills that were highly beneficial for young dancers looking to improve their technique and avoid injuries.

Next, Sarah pursued certification in acrobatics for dancers. This was a natural addition to her offerings, as acrobatics had become increasingly popular in competitive dance. By gaining this certification, she was able to offer acro classes that drew in new students interested in learning skills like handstands, cartwheels, and aerials. These classes not only boosted enrollment at her studio but also allowed her to teach a style that was in high demand, helping her fill more teaching hours.

Perhaps one of the most transformative steps in Sarah's career was earning her certification in Progressing Ballet Technique (PBT), a specialized program designed to improve dancers' core stability, strength, and alignment through the use of ballet-based exercises. PBT became a cornerstone of her teaching repertoire, as it provided her students with a solid foundation for ballet technique. Sarah's ability to integrate PBT into her regular ballet classes set her apart from other teachers, and soon, both students and parents began to seek her out specifically for her expertise in this area.

As Sarah continued to gain new certifications and develop her skills, she saw her teaching schedule grow and her reputation within the studio expand. By offering a wider variety of classes Pilates for dancers, acro, and PBT she was able to increase her teaching hours and attract a more diverse group of students. This diversification allowed her to maintain a stable, full-time teaching schedule, which was one of her initial goals.

Additionally, Sarah's efforts to expand her teaching offerings didn't go unnoticed in the wider dance community. As word spread about her unique skills and certifications, other studios began inviting her to guest teach workshops and masterclasses. Sarah embraced these opportunities, traveling to different studios and conventions to share her knowledge. These guest teaching roles not only helped her expand her network but also positioned her as an expert in her field.

By broadening her skill set and offering specialized classes, Sarah's professional growth continued to accelerate. She was no longer limited to teaching basic dance technique; she had become a well-rounded instructor who could offer students a range of classes that focused on both technical training and overall physical development.

As Sarah's reputation grew locally, she recognized the importance of establishing a personal brand that would allow her to reach a wider audience. She began to create a cohesive brand identity that reflected her expertise in multiple areas of dance and conditioning. Sarah launched her own website, where she showcased her certifications, listed her class offerings, and shared her teaching philosophy. She also created an online portfolio that featured testimonials from students and studio owners, as well as videos of her classes and workshops.

Sarah also turned to social media to build her personal brand. On platforms like Instagram and YouTube, she shared tips for dancers, PBT tutorials, and conditioning exercises that could be done at home. Her engaging content quickly attracted a following, and soon, she was receiving inquiries from dancers and studio owners across the country who were interested in her methods.

The next logical step in her career was to offer online lessons. As her social media following grew, Sarah began teaching virtual private lessons and online group classes. Her Pilates and PBT courses were especially popular with dancers who wanted to improve their technique from home. These online offerings allowed her to reach students beyond her local community and provided an additional source of income.

With her career now thriving, Sarah decided to take the leap and grow her own dance brand. She launched a series of online courses, including a program for beginner and intermediate dancers, as well as a conditioning program specifically for competitive dancers. These courses were pre-recorded and available for download, making them accessible to students around the world. Sarah's commitment to delivering high-quality educational content set her apart from others in the field, and her courses quickly gained popularity.

At this point, Sarah was not only a highly sought-after dance teacher but also a successful entrepreneur. She continued to teach at local studios, but her online courses and private lessons provided her with additional income streams, allowing her to create a sustainable and scalable career.

Reflecting on her career, Sarah credits her success to her willingness to learn new things and embrace new opportunities. "Don't limit yourself to one type of dance or teaching style," she says. "The more skills you develop, the more opportunities you'll find. I never imagined that Pilates and PBT would become such important parts of my career, but they've opened so many doors for me."

Sarah also emphasizes the importance of creating a personal brand. "In today's world, it's not enough to just be a good teacher you need to market yourself and build a brand that reflects your strengths and values. Whether you're teaching locally or reaching students online, having a strong brand helps you stand out and grow your career."

Sarah's journey highlights the power of diversification in building a successful dance career. By earning certifications in Pilates, acrobatics, and PBT, she was able to offer a wider range of classes, attract more students, and build a stable teaching schedule. Her willingness to invest in her education, embrace new opportunities, and develop a personal brand allowed her to create a multi-faceted career that continues to grow and evolve.

Today, Sarah is known not only as an exceptional dance teacher but also as an expert in dance conditioning and technique. She continues to teach at her local studio, guest teach at conventions, and grow her online presence, all while inspiring dancers to push their boundaries and develop their skills. Through her dedication and versatility, Sarah has built a thriving career in dance education that offers both personal fulfillment and professional success.

Creating a Lasting Impact by Specializing in Young Dancers Jessica's Success Story

Jessica's career began like many dance teachers, teaching a range of age groups and styles at her local studio after graduating with a dance degree. However, early on, she discovered a true passion for working with children under the age of 10. While many teachers aspired to teach older, advanced dancers, Jessica found immense joy in nurturing young dancers as they took their first steps into the world of dance.

Jessica quickly realized that her ability to connect with children and create a fun, engaging, and supportive environment was a special talent. She embraced this niche, focusing her energy on developing classes specifically designed for young dancers. This decision not only helped her find personal fulfillment but also allowed her to stand out in the competitive dance education industry.

As Jessica continued to focus on younger dancers, she began developing a curriculum that blended the foundational elements of dance with creative movement, imagination, and play. Her classes were not only about teaching technique but also about fostering creativity, confidence, and a love for movement. She incorporated storytelling, props, and age-appropriate music into her lessons, creating an environment where children could express themselves while building solid dance skills.

Jessica's approach to teaching young dancers was so successful that word quickly spread. Her classes were consistently full, and parents appreciated her ability to help their children gain confidence and a sense of belonging. Jessica's reputation for working with this age group grew, and soon she was asked to lead the recreational program at her studio.

With her specialized focus on teaching children aged 10 and under, Jessica was promoted to Recreational Director at her studio. In this role, she oversaw the studio's recreational dance programs, which included beginner and non-competitive classes for young dancers. She was responsible for creating new programs, designing curriculums, and training other teachers to implement her successful methods.

Jessica's leadership brought a fresh perspective to the studio's recreational offerings. Under her direction, the studio's enrollment grew significantly, as parents felt confident in sending their children to a program that was not only fun but also developmentally appropriate. Her unique curriculum helped create a pathway for young dancers, many of whom stayed with the studio for years, progressing into more advanced levels.

One of the key elements of Jessica's success was her ability to build strong relationships with both the children she taught and their parents. She made it a priority to communicate regularly with parents, providing updates on their child's progress and ensuring that they felt involved in the dance education process. Her nurturing and patient teaching style, combined with her emphasis on positive reinforcement, helped children feel safe and supported in the classroom.

Jessica also understood the importance of making dance accessible and fun for children, ensuring that her young students were excited to come to class each week. She emphasized personal growth, creativity, and building self-confidence, values that resonated not only with the children but also with their families.

Jessica's focus on young dancers opened up many opportunities for her. She became a sought-after instructor for early childhood dance workshops and began mentoring other teachers on how to build successful programs for younger dancers. She was invited to speak at dance teacher conferences, sharing her expertise on how to create engaging and impactful programs for preschool and elementary-aged students.

Her experience as the Recreational Director also gave her valuable leadership skills, and she continued to grow in her role by overseeing other areas of the studio, including summer camps and special events for younger dancers. Jessica's ability to focus on a niche area while also developing her leadership and business skills allowed her to build a sustainable and rewarding career.

Jessica's journey is a testament to the power of finding your passion and specializing in it. "Don't be afraid to focus on one area if that's where your heart is," she advises. "I found so much fulfillment in working with young dancers, and it has brought incredible opportunities to my career. The key is to embrace what you love and become the best at it."

By dedicating herself to working with young children and creating a curriculum that was both fun and educational, Jessica found a niche that allowed her to make a lasting impact in the dance world. Her story highlights how specializing in a specific age group or style can lead to a fulfilling and successful career in dance education.

Insights from Studio Owners: What They Look for in a Teacher

To better understand what makes a successful dance teacher, we spoke with a few studio owners who shared their perspectives on what they value most when hiring instructors.

Studio Owner 1: Me!! Nina Koch, East County Performing Arts Center

Nina emphasizes the importance of reliability and communication. "As a studio owner, I'm looking for teachers who are consistent and dependable. That means showing up on time, being prepared for every class, and following through on commitments. But it's not just about teaching skills it's also about how well they communicate with students, parents, and the rest of the studio staff. We need teachers who can build strong relationships with our dance families and create a positive, welcoming atmosphere."

Studio Owner 2: Tiffany Prout-Leitao, Center Stage Dance Academy

"To me, the most important factor is understanding their "why." It's crucial to know why they want to go into dance education, as this reveals their passion, commitment, and approach to teaching. When someone has strong personal motivation, it translates into the classroom, inspiring instruction and fostering a genuine connection with students. I have seen so many teachers go into teaching because they love to dance and grew up with it or they weren't up to the standards to make it as a professional (performer), so teaching was a back up. It becomes a job like anything else so personal motivation for dance education is a must."

Studio Owner 3: Sonya Kennedy California Dance Company

"When seeking dance teachers, I prioritize individuals who embody a growth mindset, possess a genuine passion for nurturing young hearts, and are unafraid to embrace hard work. I envision someone who gracefully learns from setbacks while boldly celebrating each success, creating an inspiring, innovative and impactful environment!"

Building a career as a dance teacher is an exciting journey with countless possibilities. The stories and insights shared in this chapter highlight just a few of the paths you can take, and they show that success doesn't have to look the same for everyone. Whether you dream of teaching at a local studio, traveling the world as a guest instructor, choreographing for big productions, or finding a niche that's all your own, there's a place for you in the dance world.

By learning from the experiences of others, staying open to new opportunities, and continually growing your skills, you can build a fulfilling and lasting career that brings joy to both you and your students. Let these stories inspire you, and remember that your journey is just as unique and valuable as those who have come before you.

Chapter 16

Practical Steps for Goal-Setting and Professional Development

As we come to the end of this book, it's time to reflect on everything you've learned and think about how you can apply these insights to your own career as a dance teacher. Throughout the chapters, we've explored the art and skill of teaching, building a personal brand, managing performances, fostering inclusivity, and much more. Now, it's your turn to take all that knowledge and turn it into action.

In this concluding chapter, we will provide a structured approach to setting professional goals and creating a personal development plan. We'll also offer practical advice on seeking out new opportunities, continuing your education, and growing your career in the dance industry. Let this chapter serve as a guide to help you reflect on your teaching journey, identify areas for growth, and map out a path to long-term success and fulfillment.

Setting clear, actionable goals is essential for growth in any career, and dance teaching is no exception. Whether you want to improve your teaching skills, take on new projects, or expand your brand, having a well-defined plan will help you stay focused and motivated. Here's a step-by-step approach to goal-setting that you can use to build your own professional development plan.

Step 1: Reflect on Your Current Position

Before setting new goals, take a moment to reflect on where you are in your career. Consider the following questions:

- What do you love most about being a dance teacher? What brings you the most joy and fulfillment?
- What are your biggest strengths as a teacher? Are there specific skills or techniques you excel at?
- What are your biggest challenges or areas where you'd like to improve?
- What are your long-term career aspirations? Where do you see yourself in the next 5 or 10 years?

This reflection will give you a clear understanding of your starting point and help you identify areas where you want to grow.

Step 2: Set Specific, Measurable Goals

When setting goals, it's important to make them specific, measurable, attainable, relevant, and time-bound (SMART). For example, instead of saying "I want to improve my teaching skills," you could set a goal like, "I want to attend two dance education workshops this year to learn new techniques for teaching beginners."

Here are some examples of SMART goals for dance teachers:

- Skill Development: "I want to improve my knowledge of contemporary dance techniques by attending a masterclass with a professional choreographer within the next six months."
- Career Advancement: "I aim to expand my brand by launching an online dance course by the end of the year."
- Personal Growth: "I plan to improve my time management by setting a weekly schedule that includes class planning, self-practice, and personal downtime."
- Network Building: "I will attend two dance conventions this year to connect with other teachers and explore guest teaching opportunities."

Step 3: Break Down Each Goal into Actionable Steps

Once you've set your goals, break each one down into smaller, actionable steps. This makes it easier to see what needs to be done and helps you track your progress. For example:

- Goal: "I want to improve my choreography skills by creating three original dance pieces this year."
- Step 1: Research different choreographic styles and techniques.
- Step 2: Dedicate time each week to practice and experiment with new movements.

- Step 3: Collaborate with a fellow dance teacher to receive feedback on the pieces.
- Step 4: Organize a small showcase or film the choreography to share on social media.

Step 4: Set Deadlines and Track Progress

Deadlines help keep you accountable and motivated. Assign a realistic timeline to each of your actionable steps, and regularly check your progress. If you find that you're falling behind, reassess your plan and make adjustments as needed. It's okay if things don't always go perfectly; the key is to stay committed and keep moving forward.

Step 5: Celebrate Your Achievements

Don't forget to celebrate your successes, no matter how small they may seem. Each accomplishment, whether it's mastering a new skill or launching a new class, is a step toward your larger goals. Acknowledge your hard work and reward yourself for your achievements this positive reinforcement will keep you motivated.

Chapter 17

Reflecting on Your Teaching Journey: Strengths, Areas for Improvement, and Growth

Reflecting on your teaching journey is an important part of professional development. By assessing your strengths, identifying areas where you can improve, and setting goals for growth, you can ensure that you're continually evolving as a dance teacher. Here are some practical ways to reflect on your career and plan for future growth.

Take a moment to think about what makes you a great teacher. Do you have a special way of connecting with younger students? Are you known for your creative choreography? Understanding your strengths can help you build on them and use them to your advantage. It can also be helpful to ask for feedback from students, parents, or colleagues who can provide insight into what they appreciate most about your teaching.

No matter how experienced you are, there's always room for growth. Identify areas where you'd like to improve, whether it's your technical knowledge, communication skills, or classroom management. Once you've identified these areas, consider how you can work on them.

Set both short-term and long-term goals for your career. Short-term goals might include things you'd like to accomplish in the next few months, while long-term goals could be what you hope to achieve in the next few years. Make sure these goals are specific and actionable, and revisit them regularly to track your progress.

Feedback is an invaluable tool for growth. Seek out feedback from students, parents, and colleagues, and be open to constructive criticism. While it can be difficult to hear, especially if it's not all positive, feedback can provide insights that help you improve. Use it as a learning opportunity and incorporate it into your development plan.

Teaching dance is demanding, both physically and emotionally. Make sure to take time to reflect on your achievements, recharge, and practice self-care. Celebrate your successes, acknowledge your hard work, and don't be afraid to take breaks when needed. Maintaining your own well-being is essential to sustaining a long and fulfilling career as a dance teacher.

The path to success as a dance teacher is not a straight line; it's a journey filled with ups, downs, and countless moments of learning and growth. Along the way, you will face challenges, but you will also experience the joy of seeing your students grow, the thrill of creating beautiful choreography, and the satisfaction of building a career around your passion for dance.

Throughout this book, we've explored different aspects of being a dance teacher from building a personal brand and managing performances to promoting inclusivity and preventing burnout. Each of these elements contributes to your success, and now, it's up to you to take the lessons you've learned and apply them to your own journey.

Set clear goals, stay open to new opportunities, and never stop learning. Be patient with yourself and remember that every dancer, every class, and every experience contributes to your growth. Your career as a dance teacher is not just about mastering technique; it's about inspiring others, sharing your love for dance, and creating a positive impact on your community.

As you move forward, keep reflecting on your progress, celebrating your successes, and seeking ways to improve. The more you invest in yourself and your development, the more fulfilling your teaching career will be. Above all, remember why you started teaching dance in the first place—your love for movement, your desire to connect with others, and your passion for sharing the art of dance. Let those reasons continue to guide you as you build a lasting, successful, and rewarding career.

Chapter 18

The Heart of Teaching Dance

Let's wrap this up! This book has guided you through the many aspects of building a successful, fulfilling career in dance education—from mastering classroom management and crafting a personal teaching style to navigating the complexities of studio ownership. But at the heart of it all is something far deeper: the passion, dedication, and love that you bring to your students and your craft every day.

Being a dance teacher is not easy. It's hard work, demanding both physically and emotionally. You spend countless hours preparing lessons, choreographing routines, and supporting your students through their struggles and triumphs. You deal with difficult conversations, long days, and sometimes heartbreak. There are moments of frustration, exhaustion, and doubt, where you might wonder if all the effort is really worth it. But then there are the moments that remind you exactly why you chose this path.

There's the joy on a student's face when they finally master a step they've been struggling with for weeks. The pride you feel when your dancers take the stage, confident and shining, performing a piece you helped them create. The connection you build with your students, who look to you not just for dance instruction but for encouragement, guidance, and inspiration.

The truth is, being a dance teacher is special because you get to make a difference every single day. You have the privilege of helping young people discover their strengths, build their confidence, and find joy through movement. You are shaping not just dancers, but individuals who learn discipline, resilience, and self-expression through the art of dance.

You see your students grow, not just as dancers, but as people. They learn to push themselves, to work hard, to be part of a team. They learn to express themselves, to take risks, to fail and try again. And you get to be a part of that journey, guiding them every step of the way.

Never underestimate the impact you have as a dance teacher. Your influence extends far beyond the studio walls. The lessons you teach about discipline, perseverance, and passion stay with your students long after they stop dancing. You're not just teaching them how to move; you're teaching them how to navigate life, to face challenges, and to find strength within themselves.

When you see your students go on to achieve their dreams, whether it's dancing professionally, teaching others, or finding success in a completely different field, you know that you played a part in their journey. That's the legacy you're building, and it's something that will last long after the music stops.

The journey of being a dance teacher is filled with ups and downs, but it's a journey worth embracing. Each day brings new challenges, but it also brings new opportunities to learn, grow, and make a difference. There will be hard days, but there will also be days of pure joy days when you see your students light up, when you watch them perform with passion and confidence, and when you know that everything you've given them has helped them become the person they are.

Being a dance teacher is not just a job; it's a calling. It requires passion, dedication, and a love for the art of dance that goes beyond words. If you have that passion, if you're willing to put in the effort, if you're ready to face the challenges head-on, then you have the power to create something truly beautiful.

To all the dance teachers reading this, know that your work is seen, appreciated, and valued. You are doing something special, something that not everyone has the courage or heart to do. You are giving your students a gift that will stay with them for the rest of their lives.

So, keep pushing, keep learning, and keep inspiring. Keep showing up, even on the hard days, because what you're doing matters. You're not just teaching dance; you're changing lives, one step at a time.

Thank you for dedicating yourself to this art, for sharing your love of dance, and for making the world a brighter place through your teaching. Whether you're building your legacy as a teacher, exploring studio ownership, or simply striving to be the best you can be, remember that your journey is unique, powerful, and worth every moment.

The dance world needs more passionate, dedicated teachers like you. So, take a deep breath, keep dancing, and never forget how much you're impacting the lives of your students. Every pirouette, every plié, every shuffle they all carry a piece of your heart, and that's what makes teaching dance so incredibly special.

Made in the USA
Columbia, SC
15 February 2025